MICHAEL CHEKHOV

Routledge Performance Practitioners is a series of introductory guides to the key theatre-makers of the last century. Each volume explains the background to and the work of one of the major influences on twentieth- and twenty-first-century performance.

These compact, well-illustrated and clearly written books will unravel the contribution of modern theatre's most charismatic innovators. *Michael Chekhov* is the first book to combine:

- A biographical introduction to Chekhov's life
- A clear explanation of his key writings
- An analysis of his work as a director
- A practical guide to Chekhov's unique actor-training exercises.

As a first step towards critical understanding, and as an initial exploration before going on to further, primary research, **Routledge Performance Practitioners** are unbeatable value for today's student.

Franc Chamberlain is a Senior Lecturer in Performance Studies at University College Northampton, and the series editor for *Routledge Performance Practitioners*.

ROUTLEDGE PERFORMANCE PRACTITIONERS

Series editor: Franc Chamberlain, University College Northampton

Routledge Performance Practitioners is an innovative series of introductory handbooks on key figures in twentieth-century performance practice. Each volume focuses on a theatre-maker whose practical and theoretical work has in some way transformed the way we understand theatre and performance. The books are carefully structured to enable the reader to gain a good grasp of the fundamental elements underpinning each practitioner's work. They will provide an inspiring springboard for future study, unpacking and explaining what can initially seem daunting.

The main sections of each book will cover:

- personal biography
- explanation of key writings
- description of significant productions
- reproduction of practical exercises.

The first volumes of the series are:

Michael Chekhov by Franc Chamberlain
Jacques Lecoq by Simon Murray
Vsevolod Meyerhold by Jonathan Pitches
Konstantin Stanislavsky by Bella Merlin

Future volumes will include:

Eugenio Barba
Pina Bausch
Augusto Boal
Bertolt Brecht
Peter Brook
Jerzy Grotowski
Anna Halprin
Joan Littlewood
Ariane Mnouchkine

MICHAEL CHEKHOV

Franc Chamberlain

Routledge
Taylor & Francis Group

LONDON AND NEW YORK

First published 2004
by Routledge
11 New Fetter Lane, London EC4P 4EE

Simultaneously published in the USA and Canada
by Routledge
29 West 35th Street, New York, NY 10001

Routledge is an imprint of the Taylor & Francis Group

Typeset in Perpetua by
Florence Production Ltd, Stoodleigh, Devon
Printed and bound in Great Britain by
TJ International Ltd, Padstow, Cornwall

British Library Cataloguing in Publication Data
A catalogue record for this book is available from
the British Library

Library of Congress Cataloging in Publication Data
Chamberlain, Franc.
    Michael Chekhov/Franc Chamberlain.
        p. cm. – (Routledge performance practitioners)
        1. Chekhov, Michael, 1891–1955 – Criticism and
    interpretation.   2. Acting.   I. Title.   II. Series.
    PN2728.C45C48 2003
    792'.028'092 – dc21   2003004230

ISBN 0–415–25877–4 (hbk)
ISBN 0–415–25878–2 (pbk)

TO MY PARENTS,
FREDERICK AND ROGELIA

CONTENTS

FIGURES

All images courtesy of the Dartington Hall Trust Archive.

ACKNOWLEDGEMENTS

I gratefully acknowledge the permission of the Dartington Hall Trust Archive to reproduce the photographs contained in this volume, and to quote from manuscripts held in the archive. I'm also grateful to Yvonne Widger, administrator of the archive and collection at the Trust, for her assistance during my time at the archive and by telephone.

Talia Rodgers has been a supportive and challenging editor, waiting patiently as I tried to juggle the writing of this book with the editing of the *Routledge Performance Practitioners* series. I wish these had been the only two things to juggle! Cheerful and able support was also offered by Rosie Waters and Diane Parker at Routledge.

Thank you to Simon Blaxland-Delange for permission to quote from his not-yet-published translation of Michael Chekhov's autobiography.

During 2001 I received funding to research and write this book from the Arts and Humanities Research Board and from the School of Cultural Studies at University College Northampton. I hope this is evidence that I spent my time in a worthwhile manner.

I'm grateful to all of those people who've participated in my classes and explored Chekhov with me over the years. You are too many to name, but thank you. Thanks are also due to the following people who have assisted with this book in various ways (although they may not always have known it): Jane Bacon, Bob Godfrey, Jonathan Pitches, Anthony Shrubsall, Rob Daniels, Martin Sharp, Robert Ellerman, Ralph

Yarrow, George Savona, Arlene Audergon, Lucy Smith, Phelim McDermott, Jane Turner, Jytte Vikkelsoe, Francis Batten and Frances Babbage. Thank you also to Sarah Moore and the staff at Florence Production.

Finally, I would like to thank all the teachers and students of Chekhov's work who have helped me in my learning, including Mala Powers, Jack Colvin, Joanna Merlin, Deirdre Hurst du Prey, Mary-Lou Taylor, Hurd Hatfield, Ford Rainey, Daphne Field, Paul Rogers, Sarah Kane, Lendley Black, Andrei Kirillov, Marina Ivanova, Liisa Byckling, David Zinder, Per Brahe, Graham Dixon, Lenard Petit, Jobst Langhans and Lisa Patton.

BIOGRAPHY
AND CONTEXT

Michael Chekhov, regarded as a phenomenal actor by many who saw him, is one of the key figures in twentieth-century theatre. His ability to transform himself onstage was celebrated by some of the major directors of the century: Stanislavsky, Vakhtangov, Reinhardt and Meyerhold, and his practical advice continues to inspire actors through his writings and through schools devoted to his work in Russia, Lithuania, Holland, Denmark, Germany, Great Britain and the US. His book, *To the Actor*, is considered one of the best actor-training manuals ever published in the European tradition. Yet in spite of this there have been very few studies of his work published in any language.

CHILDHOOD

Mikhail (Michael) Aleksandrovich Chekhov was born in St Petersburg, Russia, on 16 August 1891. His father Aleksandr, the brother of the great playwright, **Anton Chekhov**, was an eccentric and an inventor. Aleksandr Chekhov was always dreaming up some scheme or experiment, often in order to save money, and involving young Michael in much of the labour. Chekhov respected and admired his father for his intelligence and his creativity, but lamented the time spent helping with his father's experiments when he felt that he should have been playing.

On the positive side Aleksandr would talk to his young son about a wide range of subjects, including philosophy, natural history, medicine and maths.

One skill that Aleksandr possessed, which gave much delight to his son, was the ability to draw cartoons and capture the essence of a person's character in a few lines. Michael considered that his own love of cartoons had an important effect on his later development. Cartoon caricatures emphasise a recognisable aspect of a person and exaggerate it until it appears ridiculous. A good caricaturist can make the individual recognisable through this exaggeration and also bring out an aspect of the person which is not usually noticed. Chekhov developed a healthy sense of the ridiculous, or the grotesque, and felt that this was very important for the actor, because it brought a sense of humour and lightheartedness into work that might otherwise have become self-indulgent.

Anton Chekhov (1860–1904): Russian playwright whose major works *The Seagull* (1896), *Uncle Vanya* (1899), *The Three Sisters* (1901) and *The Cherry Orchard* (1904) were all staged by Stanislavsky at the Moscow Art Theatre. Chekhov's plays involve very little action and there is a strong emphasis on mood and atmosphere. Although Chekhov was unhappy with the naturalistic detail of Stanislavsky's productions, it is largely due to the work of the Moscow Art Theatre that these plays have become central to the study of twentieth-century drama.

A major problem in Chekhov's relationship with his father was that Aleksandr was an alcoholic and had an inability to harness his immense energy and talents in any purposeful direction. When Michael was a young man he also became an alcoholic and found himself unable to work systematically. The recollections of his childhood presented in his autobiography, *The Path of the Actor* (1928), suggest the importance of finding a balance between work and play, between spontaneity and discipline. With his father's constant demands that he work, the young Chekhov's life was skewed away from play, and in his young adulthood he swung the other way and emphasised play. This, as we shall see, was to cause him some problems with Stanislavsky at the Moscow Art Theatre.

PERFORMANCE BEGINNINGS

Chekhov's first performances were for his mother and nanny, Aleksandr being much less interested in his son's performances. The self-devised shows often featured the members of this intimate circle as the key figures who would be involved in both realistic and fantastic situations. At this early stage there was no sense that Chekhov would become an actor and he thought that he would become a doctor or a fireman. Later, as he began to perform extracts from Dickens and other authors, with some of his own material incorporated, for his family and guests, he became more aware of the possibility of becoming an actor and joined a local amateur dramatic group before moving on to drama school.

CHEKHOV AT THE MALY

FROM IMITATION TO CREATION

In 1907, aged sixteen, Chekhov joined the Suvorin Theatre school, which was attached to the famous Maly Suvorinsky Theatre in St Petersburg. Two of his teachers at the Maly, B.S. Glagolin and N.N. Arbatov, were to make an impression on him and influence his later thinking on the theatre, although not necessarily in the way that they intended. Glagolin was a talented actor and it was while watching him in the role of Khlestakov in *The Government Inspector* in 1909 that Chekhov had the insight that:

> Glagolin played Khlestakov *not like everyone else*, although I had never seen anyone in this role before Glagolin. This feeling of 'not like everyone else' arose in me without any comparisons or analogies directly from Glagolin's acting. The unusual *freedom* and originality of his creativity in this role astonished me, and I was not mistaken: no-one played Khlestakov in the way Glagolin did.
>
> (Chekhov 1927: 16)

What does Chekhov mean by the statement that Glagolin played 'not like everyone else'? In one sense it is obvious. Any actor necessarily brings personal difference to a role and Mel Gibson's Hamlet is very different from Ethan Hawke's or Laurence Olivier's. Chekhov, however, began to think about why this was. For him it wasn't as simple as answering 'because they're different people'. He was later to put forward the idea of 'creative individuality' as his answer. One of the aspects of creative individuality is a sense of creative freedom and Chekhov was also interested in the freedom with which Glagolin played. Chekhov found Glagolin interesting, because there was no attempt to copy the role as it had been played by other performers.

The tradition within the drama schools at this time was that students would imitate the way that their teachers performed. Chekhov later argued that this meant that the students didn't get a grasp of the fundamental principles of the art of acting. That is, they only learned to imitate and not to create. The lesson Chekhov took from Glagolin's performance, whether it was intended or not, was that the actor doesn't need to be an imitator but can be a creative artist. This is an important key to Chekhov's view of the actor.

ARTISTIC FREEDOM AND FORM

One of the fundamental principles that Chekhov thought was lacking in the curricula of the drama schools was an understanding of artistic form. This sense of form is something which is central not only to the art of the actor but to the whole process of staging from Chekhov's viewpoint. It was Glagolin's colleague, Arbatov, who impressed on Chekhov the importance of this principle. Chekhov was critical of the naturalistic style of Arbatov's productions, claiming that naturalism was the absence of style and therefore of art. But he valued Arbatov's grasp of form in the overall shape and design of the performance, in his models and even in the arrangement of his study.

Chekhov became critical of the haphazard curricula of the drama schools which failed to educate their students in the basic principles of the art of the theatre. Without an understanding of form and style Chekhov felt that the actor was either confined to imitating old forms or working without any form at all. This working without form was later described by Chekhov as being a false freedom. The performer lacks artistic discipline and Chekhov, drawing on his own experience, suggested that a lack of artistic discipline implies a lack of discipline in everyday life; that is a failure to understand the conditional nature of freedom. Chekhov believed that there were important connections between the actor's life and his or her profession. He was very critical of actors who felt that they didn't have to study even the fundamentals of acting because their natural talent would show them what to do.

He caricatures such actors as believing that study would only stifle their spontaneity. On the other hand, Chekhov only came to this realisation in the 1920s and criticises himself for putting too much emphasis on his own talent and not seeing the value of working systematically to master the craft of acting earlier in his career.

After graduating from the school, Chekhov joined the company of the Maly Suvorinsky Theatre and played a variety of roles, both in performances in St Petersburg and on tour.

PUTTING ON A SHOW

While Chekhov was at the Maly, however, his father's health began to deteriorate and his own inner conflict led to him drinking more and more heavily and performing while drunk. Chekhov described himself during this period as someone who was always 'putting on a show', whether onstage or off. He was using the theatre as a way of hiding from his personal problems, not least his alcoholism. Hiding from our problems in a fantasy world is not helpful in the long run, even if it brings some temporary relief, because the problems tend not to go away and can often get worse. In terms of the theatre, an actor who is always 'putting on a show' is likely to keep repeating old habits, and to perform just for the approval of the audience. There is also the risk that, if we're hiding from ourselves, we're not really able to make good contact with our fellow performers or the deeper sources of our creativity. In other words we avoid the challenges to developing the sensitivity necessary for becoming an effective performer. It took several difficult years before Chekhov realised that he had to face his problems.

THE MOSCOW ART THEATRE

MEETING STANISLAVSKY

It was at this moment of decline that his aunt **Olga Knipper-Chekhova**, who was visiting St Petersburg with the **Moscow Art Theatre**, suggested that he join them. She promised to discuss the matter with **Stanislavsky**. Chekhov was given a preliminary audition by Vishnevsky, one of the leading MAT actors, and the following day was auditioned by Stanislavsky himself. Chekhov describes it as a rather

Olga Knipper-Chekhova (1868–1959): Russian actress who was one of the original members of the Moscow Art Theatre and who married Anton Chekhov in 1901. She played leading roles in all of Anton Chekhov's plays staged at the MAT, as well as major roles in other key productions.

Moscow Art Theatre (MAT): Inspired by small art theatres that had sprung up in Europe during the previous ten years, the MAT quickly became one of the most celebrated theatres in the world.

Konstantin Stanislavsky (1863–1938): Russian actor, teacher, director and founder, with Vladimir Nemirovich-Danchenko (1858–1943), of the Moscow Art Theatre in 1898. Stanislavsky's work is usually associated with realism in both staging and acting, but he also experimented with different styles of theatre.

traumatic encounter – he was nervous to be in the presence of such a celebrated director and was unable to talk freely. He answered all of Stanislavsky's questions mechanically, then, when he was invited to do his audition speech, his collar suddenly snapped and the edges bit into his cheek. Not surprisingly he was embarrassed and wanted to run away, but froze. After a few moments he realised that it couldn't get much worse and was able to relax into his piece. Although we can assume that Stanislavsky wasn't being overly generous because of his connections with Chekhov's family, the audition was a success and Chekhov was invited to join the theatre on 16 June 1912. Stanislavsky's notes after the audition included the comments 'talented, has charm. One of the real hopes for the future' (Benedetti 1990: 207).

LOOKING FOR A NEW THEATRE

Michael Chekhov was only seven years old when Nemirovich-Danchenko and Stanislavsky formed the Moscow Art Theatre in 1898 and included his uncle's play *The Seagull* in their first season. Stanislavsky's approach, at this time, was to attempt to create as detailed an imitation of life onstage as possible. A counter movement to Stanislavsky's **realism** was **symbolism**, which was championed in Russia at this time by such practitioners as **Vsevolod Meyerhold**. Meyerhold, inspired by the symbolist plays and theories of **Maeterlinck**, was interested in the idea of a stylised theatre which emphasised 'atmosphere' or 'mood' over naturalistic detail. It is important to note that Anton Chekhov himself was uncertain of Stanislavsky's approach to his plays.

Atmosphere, for Meyerhold, was generated by the actors and, despite his reservations regarding Stanislavsky's production values, he felt that the MAT actors had managed to evoke the appropriate mood of *The Seagull*. Working with these symbolist influences for a decade, Meyerhold attempted several productions of Maeterlinck, searching for a technique which would use movement as 'plastic music' in order to construct an 'external depiction of an inner experience' (Braun 1978: 36).

The themes of atmosphere, actors' creativity and physicalisation of inner experience, as well as the question of style, which were to become important elements in Michael Chekhov's method, can be seen to have been part of the theatrical milieu for over a decade before 1912 when he joined the MAT.

Realism: an artistic movement which focuses on everyday life and naturalistic detail. Requires a naturalistic and psychological approach to staging/acting.

Symbolism: an artistic movement which emphasised suggestion and atmosphere, attempting to represent the inner world of dreams and imagination rather than everyday 'outer' reality. Requires a stylised approach to staging/acting.

Vsevolod Meyerhold (1874–1940): Russian actor and director who was one of the original members of the MAT but who became opposed to Stanislavsky's realist approach. Meyerhold's creative and imaginative explorations were to lead him beyond symbolism to a rhythmical physical theatre.

Maurice Maeterlinck (1862–1949): Belgian symbolist playwright who was a key figure in the development of a non-naturalistic European theatre. The emphasis on silence, stillness and mysterious dreamlike happenings in his plays required a new kind of staging and acting. His plays are rarely staged nowadays, but he had a major impact on the development away from naturalistic theatre both in text and performance.

Edward Gordon Craig (1872–1966): English actor, designer, director, theorist and artist, whose aim was to create a non-naturalistic theatre. He argued that puppets were more artistic than most live performers, but looked forward to a theatre based on movement which would be created by actor-artists. Author of *On the Art of the Theatre* (1911), a major contribution to twentieth-century theatrical thinking.

CHEKHOV AND CRAIG

Chekhov's first role at the MAT was as a crowd member in the riot scene in the production of *Hamlet* which was a result of the collaboration between Stanislavsky and the great English theatre artist **Edward Gordon Craig**. Craig was one of the most celebrated and controversial theatre practitioners of the period. He was opposed to naturalism and realism in the theatre and the collaboration with Stanislavsky was fraught with problems. Craig wanted imagination to replace imitation on the stage and felt that the theatre should have more in common with a dream than a representation of everyday life. Although Craig is often represented as someone who was opposed to actors, he wanted actors to become creative artists in their own right and felt that Stanislavsky didn't give actors sufficient freedom to improvise (Innes 1998: 49).

Chekhov barely mentions Craig in his writings, but he almost certainly read Craig's *On the Art of the Theatre* and he would have had some insight into Craig's aims through his involvement in *Hamlet*. Craig's interest in improvisation and the actor's creativity, movement and imagination, as well as his interest in the spiritual dimension of theatre, is very much in line with Chekhov's own.

THE FIRST STUDIO

The search for a new approach to acting which would emphasise the creativity of the actor was being undertaken across Europe. Stanislavsky had always aimed to break the fixed habits of actors and to develop acting as a creative art. By the time Michael Chekhov joined the MAT, Stanislavsky was already exploring new directions and the work with Craig was part of this. The most significant project, however, was the establishment of the experimental First Studio in 1912 under **Leopold Sulerzhitsky**.

Teaching at the Studio was carried out by Stanislavsky himself, Leopold Sulerzhitsky and the brilliantly talented **Evgeny Vakhtangov**. The Studio included Chekhov, **Richard Boleslavsky** and **Maria Ouspenskaya** among its members. Boleslavsky decided to undertake a production of Herman Heijermans' *The Wreck of the 'Good Hope'* (1913) and, after several months' work, was encouraged by Stanislavsky to present it before an audience of relatives and friends.

It was in *The Wreck of the 'Good Hope'* that Chekhov first drew critical attention, when he transformed the minor role of Kobe from a stereo-typical 'idiot fisherman' into a 'sincere and morbid seeker of the truth' (Gordon 1987: 119). When his interpretation of the role was challenged on the grounds that it wasn't what the playwright had intended, Chekhov asserted his creative individuality, claiming that he had found the 'true' character by going beyond both text and author.

Boleslavsky's production was followed by Vakhtangov's of *The Festival of Peace* (1913), the adaptation of Charles Dickens' *The Cricket on the Hearth* (1915), directed by Sushkevich, and Vakhtangov's production of Henning Berger's *The Deluge* (1915), creations which established the reputation of the First Studio. Chekhov played significant roles in all three of these productions. In *The Festival of Peace* he played an alcoholic, Fribe, and envisioned him as a man for whom each part of his body was dying a distinct death. This was followed by his interpretation of the role of Caleb, a gentle but frightened toymaker, in *The Cricket on the Hearth* – a performance highly praised by Stanislavsky among others. Chekhov and Sulerzhitsky made all of the mechanical toys for the production, which gives some indication of the extent of Chekhov's involvement in the Studio. He was, however, plagued by inner conflict and unable to engage with as many of the Studio's activities as he wished. Writing that he was 'unable to understand why on earth all

---

Leopold Sulerzhitsky (1872–1916): a pacifist who was imprisoned in 1896 for refusing military service. Introduced to Stanislavsky in 1900, he had become his personal assistant by 1907, and then the head of the First Studio at its opening in 1912. Sulerzhitsky introduced a form of yoga into western actor training.

Evgeny Vakhtangov (1883–1923): brilliant member of the MAT who attempted to bring together the work of Stanislavsky and Meyerhold in his 'fantastic realism'. Vakhtangov had an incredible period of creativity just before he died, directing Michael Chekhov in one of his greatest roles, Erik XIV, as well as major productions of *Turandot* and *The Dybbuk* (both in 1922).

Richard Boleslavsky (1889–1937) and Maria Ouspenskaya (1876–1949): two members of the MAT Studio who remained in the US after a tour in 1923. They became the main teachers at the American Laboratory Theatre which had considerable impact on the way in which Stanislavsky's teachings developed in America. Both had successful Hollywood careers.

that was being done around me with such love and care was necessary' (1927: 23), Chekhov indicates his state of mind, but also indicates a familiar attitude among young actors who just want to act and do their part and not really be involved in all of the other work that is necessary for the staging of a performance.

As part of the First Studio, Chekhov developed his skills in the basic elements of Stanislavsky's method: relaxation, concentration, naivety, imagination, communication and affective memory. Chekhov was eventually to reject Stanislavsky's emphasis on memory, but the other aspects of the Studio's work were to find a place in his own method, although somewhat transformed.

CHEKHOV AND VAKHTANGOV

In *The Deluge* Chekhov and Vakhtangov shared the role of Frazer and audiences got the opportunity to compare and contrast the performances of the two most exciting young actors of the Studio in the same role. Chekhov's performance was criticised for being too grotesquely physical, but it was nonetheless an interpretation which also won a considerable number of admirers. There is a story that Vakhtangov began to perform Frazer in a similar manner. It is difficult to establish whether Vakhtangov took the outer form of Chekhov's interpretation and filled it with his own imagination, or whether he took a similar approach to Chekhov but came up with his own, distinct, physical score. Given that Chekhov, like Stanislavsky, was interested in the individual actor's unique creativity, and also given his great admiration for Vakhtangov, it seems likely that Vakhtangov's amended interpretation was inspired by Chekhov's work rather than being a direct copy.

During his time at the First Studio, Chekhov built a strong friendship with Vakhtangov. There are numerous stories of their friendship, but one which is often repeated is the story of a game they used to play together when they shared a room on tour. You might be familiar with a game called 'Master and Slave', in which the slave has to carry out the master's wishes, whatever they are. Chekhov and Vakhtangov's slave in their version was an ape. They took it in turns to play the ape, which had to carry out all of the household chores and whatever else the master wanted him to do. The ape was to do most things on all fours. If the master was displeased with the ape, then he could beat him. One day, however, they took it too far and the game ended in a fight in which Chekhov lost a tooth! Chekhov was later to be critical of how actors at the Studio believed that it was necessary to lose themselves in the part and this is a good example of two of the company's leading actors playing it 'for real'. Both Chekhov and Vakhtangov were to become concerned in their work to find an appropriate physical, emotional and psychological balance in performance without losing the sense that they were making theatre.

TROUBLE WITH IMPROVISATION

Between 1912 and 1918 Chekhov developed his reputation as a talented actor in a number of roles, despite occasional conflicts with Stanislavsky and some of the other members of the company. Part of the problem appears to have been the expression of his actor's creativity. In one of his earliest roles at the MAT, in *Le Malade imaginaire*, Chekhov was criticised by Stanislavsky for having too much fun with the role and Chekhov himself describes how the fun, which started out as creative exploration, ended by undermining the performance. A group of actors was given the task of constructing a comic interlude for the play and encouraged to find ways of making the audience laugh; one of their responses was to bet on who would make the audience laugh most during any particular performance. The difficulty arose when the actors began to laugh as well, so Stanislavsky stepped in to stop them experimenting further.

Humour enables us to create a distance from both the work and ourselves and this enables us to become more objective. Chekhov argued that we need to be objective in order to create good representations on the stage. This sense of humour is, however, to be distinguished from the uncontrolled need to laugh at any opportunity. Chekhov suffered from this defect and records that he was occasionally guilty of bursting into spontaneous laughter in the middle of a performance (what we call 'corpsing'). He came to regard this as an insult to the audience. There is a distinction here between the humour which enables us to represent even the most serious subjects with a light touch, assisting us in going deeper into them, and laughter which undermines the whole process of the performance.

DEEPENING CRISIS

The image we get of Chekhov during his time at the Moscow Art Theatre is of an immensely talented actor who is always taking things to extremes. Throughout the years 1912–18 things got steadily worse.

At the end of his first season at the MAT, Chekhov returned to visit his parents and watched his father die of throat cancer – this led him to some reflections on the representation of death on the stage. He criticised the attempt to merely imitate the physiological processes of dying on stage, because, as we have already noted, he didn't think that naturalism was an art. Chekhov focused on the rhythmical pattern of dying. He suggested that the actor representing a dying person needed to find a way of constructing the rhythm of the role, so that the audience had a sense of time gradually slowing down until there was a complete stop.

The death of his father, however, intensified Chekhov's personal difficulties and, as he moved deeper into his personal crisis, his work began to suffer. Chekhov was unable to give up drinking and became obsessed by thoughts that his mother was in danger. He became increasingly afraid on her account and this developed into more and more fear in general. What Chekhov was experiencing at this time was the power of the imagination to supply oppressive images and how alcohol abuse can reinforce these negative images. By 1916 Chekhov was moving

> **The Russian Revolution**: Russia was ruled by a hereditary monarchy and moves towards democracy were ruthlessly suppressed. The First World War (1914–18) caused serious problems and the Tsar was forced to abdicate in March 1917. The provisional government failed to solve the economic problems and was overthrown by a communist revolution headed by Lenin. This sparked a civil war in Russia which lasted until 1920, caused many deaths and had a serious impact on the quality of people's lives. In 1923, with the communists victorious, the former Russian Empire became the Union of Soviet Socialist Republics.

towards a physical and psychological collapse. He was trapped in a vicious circle of oppressive and destructive fantasies and behaviours, especially his excessive drinking.

The Russian Revolution of October 1917, which had an immense impact on all aspects of life in Russia and was eventually to lead to Chekhov's exile from his homeland, is hardly mentioned in Chekhov's writings. We know that he was opposed to violent revolution on the grounds that violence only led to more violence and suffering. Certainly his personal difficulties intensified immediately after the revolution. By 1918, he was drinking heavily, his wife had divorced him and taken their daughter away, his cousin had committed suicide using Chekhov's gun, his mother had died and he was sinking into suicidal depression. He was unable to act and on one occasion left the stage in the middle of a performance.

RECOVERY

Interpreting his extreme state as a spiritual crisis, Chekhov began to investigate the anthroposophy, or spiritual science, of **Rudolf Steiner**, which was attracting the interest of a number of Russian artists, including the poet, novelist and playwright, **Andrei Bely**, and **Wassily Kandinsky**. Steiner's relevance to Michael Chekhov is twofold. First, he offered a model of the human being and of spiritual development that was useful to Chekhov, both in his personal life and in his understanding of the art of acting. Second, Steiner was very much involved in performance and, as well as writing and producing plays,

Rudolf Steiner (1861–1925): Austrian philosopher who stressed the importance of intuitive spiritual knowledge in his system of thought and teaching which he called anthroposophy. Steiner believed that the arts, including theatre, were an important aid to spiritual development. His theories of education led to the foundation of Waldorf schools around the world and the Camp Hill communities for young people with learning difficulties. Steiner was also influential in the development of organic farming and homeopathy.

Andrei Bely (1880–1934): Russian symbolist poet, novelist and playwright whose novel *Petersburg* (1916) is regarded as one of the masterpieces of twentieth-century literature.

Wassily Kandinsky (1866–1944): one of the founders of abstract painting who was also a poet, playwright and author of the influential *Concerning the Spiritual in Art* (1912).

he developed a system of movement, **eurythmy**, as well as an approach to speech as invisible gesture.

Steiner, like others before him, drew a distinction between the everyday self, with which we normally identify, and the 'higher ego' which is our more authentic and creative self. Anthroposophy enabled Chekhov to gain a distance from his personal troubles and to put them in a different perspective, from which he saw himself as a 'drunken egotist' (Gordon 1987: 124). He began an intense study of Steiner's teachings as a means of liberation from his self-indulgent and self-destructive tendencies. Steiner's theories were to form the basis of Chekhov's personal belief and to have a significant impact on his theory of the actor.

AGAINST EMOTION MEMORY

It is after 1918 that Chekhov comes out most strongly against Stanislavsky's use of personal experience and emotion, arguing that this, in effect, binds the actor to the habits of the everyday self, which was not the way to liberate the actor's creativity. Furthermore, Chekhov argued that the emphasis should be on the character's feelings, not the actor's – not 'how would I feel' but 'what does the character feel' – and that this would enable the actor to transform into the character rather than reducing the character to the personality of the actor.

Chekhov gives a very good example of what he means by this. In a scene where a character's child is ill, the Stanislavskian actor will behave as if this were their own child. This adapts the character to the actor's life and patterns of feeling and behaviour. The Chekhovian actor, on the other hand, will focus on the character and observe how the character responds to the child and behave in that way. In this case the actor is adapting to the character.

Chekhov interpreted Steiner's higher ego as the 'artist in us that stands behind all of our creative processes' (Chekhov 1991: 16) and believed it was the key to this approach. Chekhov eventually identified four ways in which a sensitivity to this higher ego would help the actor's work: (1) it was the source of the actor's 'creative individuality', which explained why different actors played the same role differently, and helped the actor to go beyond the text; (2) it was possessed of an ethical sense which enabled the actor to feel the conflict between 'good' and 'evil' in the play; (3) it enabled a sensitivity to the audience's perspective on the play in performance; and (4) it brought a sense of detachment, compassion and humour into the actor's work by conferring freedom from the 'narrow, selfish ego' (Chekhov 1991: 24).

Chekhov also drew on Steiner's explorations into movement and speech through eurythmy and on his theories of speech as invisible gesture and these found their way into his system. Once the work of Steiner was added to the influences from the Moscow Art Theatre and his own reflections on the actor's art, Chekhov began to construct a coherent system of training distinct from Stanislavsky's. Between 1918 and 1921 he ran workshops in his flat in Moscow to explore the

---

Eurythmy: a system of movement developed by Steiner in which sounds are given specific physical postures. In this way, sounds are 'made visible' and poems, for example could be turned into movement sequences. (It must not be confused with eurhythmics.) Steiner's work on speech as invisible gesture is this process in reverse, where the performer in the act of speaking is making an inner gesture.

possibilities opened up by his new interests, although these experiments were only popular with a minority and financial difficulties led to closure. Chekhov's recovery from his illness led to his blossoming as an actor and, from 1921 to 1927, he performed a number of major roles at the First Studio (which became the Second Moscow Art Theatre in 1924) and at the MAT which confirmed his exceptional talent.

DISCIPLINE AND SPONTANEITY

Part of Chekhov's recovery and reorientation included his turn against the idea that natural talent was enough for an actor to be successful as a creative artist. The actor had to be willing to work extremely hard in order to develop any apparently 'natural' talent. Any failure to commit to this work would lead to the actor being left behind as the art of the theatre continued to evolve. Talent that wasn't worked on was doomed to fade and die.

That Chekhov should not have come to recognise the importance of the relationship between hard work and spontaneity until after he stopped working with Stanislavsky suggests not only why he had so many difficulties at the MAT, but also something of his talent. Without the change of attitude that occurred after 1918, Chekhov might be remembered just as a promising actor who self-destructed.

VAKHTANGOV'S FANTASTIC REALISM

Vakhtangov was initially very taken by Stanislavsky's notion of emotion memory, but eventually argued for a combination of Stanislavsky and Meyerhold which he called 'fantastic realism'. Vakhtangov felt that Stanislavsky was too attached to naturalism and missed the significance of theatricality in the theatre, while Meyerhold's fascination with stylised physicality had led him to ignore the importance of feelings; it was necessary to combine both approaches to create a theatre which was both 'live' and 'theatrical' (Cole and Chinoy 1963: 185–91).

One of Chekhov's major acting triumphs was when he appeared in the leading roles in Vakhtangov's production of Strindberg's *Erik XIV* at the First Studio in 1921. *Erik XIV* tells the story of a weak and deranged sixteenth-century Swedish king, who imprisons and murders the nobility, is deposed in a rebellion led by his brothers and, after marrying his mistress, attempts to flee the country. Strindberg saw Erik as a Swedish Hamlet and Chekhov's Erik XIV was full of internal conflict which was revealed through sharp contrasts in physical and vocal dynamics. He would, for example, move sharply from a whisper to a loud cry, or from a timid movement to a strong, bold one, but always with a clear sense of rhythm and form that was said to have the clarity of a drawing.

Looking for a physical means to represent the weakness of the character, Chekhov was inspired by Vakhtangov, who visualised Erik trapped within a circle from which he constantly tried to escape. Stretching out his hands beyond the circle in hope, Erik would find nothing and leave his hands dangling in misery. Chekhov felt that the essence of Erik's character was expressed in Vakhtangov's gesture and claimed that, from that moment, he had no difficulty in playing the character, with all of the appropriate nuances, throughout the whole of the play (Chekhov 1991: 89). Linked to this gesture, for Chekhov, was the image of 'an eagle with a broken wing' (Powers 2002: xxxii). This condensation of the essence of the character into a single full-body gesture is the prototype of Chekhov's 'psychological gesture' (see Chapter 2) and he reports another example from his work with Stanislavsky on Gogol's *The Government Inspector* at the MAT in the same year.

STANISLAVSKY, CHEKHOV AND *THE GOVERNMENT INSPECTOR*

Chekhov describes a rehearsal with Stanislavsky where the director is giving him suggestions for playing Khlestakov and 'suddenly made a lightning-quick movement with his arms and hands, as if throwing them up and at the same time vibrating with his fingers, elbows, and even his shoulders' (Chekhov 1991: 89). Once again Chekhov understood the whole of the role from this condensation. What both of these incidents show is that the idea of expressing the essence of the role in a gesture was familiar to Stanislavsky and Vakhtangov and that the idea isn't Chekhov's as such. Nonetheless he was the one who developed the idea of the Psychological Gesture and made it an important aspect of his training as an intuitive rather than an analytical approach to character.

In contrast to the brooding melancholy of Erik, Chekhov's Khlestakov in *The Government Inspector* was light and mischievous.

Chekhov imagined that Khlestakov had bedsprings tied to the soles of his feet (Powers 2002: xxxii). Critics were stunned by the scene in which Khlestakov improvises fantastic lies in the Mayor's house, because Chekhov would play it differently each night. Opening to the higher ego involved a means of accessing the creativity and spontaneity that Stanislavsky had been searching for and provided an alternative approach to his creative state of mind. The problem for Chekhov was that, when creative energy was unleashed, the actor was inclined to overstep necessary boundaries and there was a need to develop a way of ensuring that the limits of the performance were respected. By the time of the performance Chekhov was able to keep the basic shape of the scene, but earlier in rehearsals he had got so carried away while improvising with an apple that he lost contact with the objective of the scene and the other actors before Stanislavsky called a halt. The ability to improvise within set limits was another aspect of the performer which Chekhov wanted to develop through his teaching (du Prey 1983: 89).

CHEKHOV AT THE SECOND MAT

Vakhtangov died in 1922 and Chekhov was offered the directorship of the First Studio, which became the Second MAT in 1924. Chekhov continued to act as well as to teach and direct and in the 1924–5 season he directed and performed the title role in a critically acclaimed production of *Hamlet*. One of the key moments in the production was the appearance of Hamlet's father's ghost. Chekhov chose not to have another actor play the ghost but to use his imagination to project an image outside of himself and then respond to it. This was so successful that some members of the audience claimed to be able to see the ghost.

In this way Chekhov was attempting to solve one of the key problems in non-naturalistic theatre of the late nineteenth and early twentieth centuries: how to stage the supernatural. This had caused great problems for Stanislavsky and his failure to deal successfully with the supernatural elements of Maeterlinck's *The Intruder* resulted in him inviting Meyerhold to attempt a studio production. Meyerhold's production of Maeterlinck's *The Death of Tintagiles* in 1905 was also deemed unsuccessful and Stanislavsky's attempts to find a way out of naturalism led to his collaboration on *Hamlet* with Craig.

In his collection of essays *On the Art of the Theatre* (1911), Craig had written of the ghosts in Shakespeare's tragedies as the keynote of the performance and was unhappy with the contemporary attempts to stage them. Craig suggested that, while we might feel the presence of the ghosts when we read the plays, we feel nothing when they appear on the stage. Whatever the stage technology used – gauzes, lighting or winches – he felt that the ghosts remained too solid and that a way had to be found to achieve a sense of otherworldliness. Stanislavsky had invited Craig to work with him in 1908, but the production didn't open until 1912 and, despite critical acclaim, neither Craig nor Stanislavsky was satisfied with the results. Vakhtangov had a small part in the Craig/Stanislavsky *Hamlet* and Craig felt that he was one of only two people who really understood his conception of theatre. Chekhov's first stage appearance at the MAT was as a crowd member in this production and this experience, together with his relationship with Vakhtangov, will have contributed to his conception of *Hamlet* and his radical staging of the encounters with the ghost. The ability to act with an invisible partner is an essential skill for contemporary film-making, where special effects can mean that the actor has nothing but imagination to work with.

Despite the acclaim Chekhov received for *Hamlet*, however, it was the method of staging the ghost and his innovative rehearsal practices which contributed to his reputation as someone with 'mystical tendencies', a dangerous charge in the Soviet Union. In 1927 there was conflict within the Second MAT and sixteen members of the company quit in protest at Chekhov's approach. What were the kinds of things that upset them? That Chekhov had them juggling balls while rehearsing in order to get a sense of rhythm and ensemble, and also that he was conducting experiments with archetypal images in order to approach the character's ego.

THE PATH OF THE ACTOR

In 1928, at the age of thirty-six, Chekhov published his artistic auto-biography entitled *The Path of the Actor*, which describes a sense of disappointment with the state of the theatre in the early 1920s and his personal shame as an actor in participating in what he perceived as a 'great lie'. *The Path of the Actor* was an attempt to look at his life up to 1927 and to cast an eye to the future, towards the direction of his own journey and that which was necessary for the theatre if it was to become an effectively revitalised art.

Chekhov, writing in the *Path of the Actor*, claims that actors have no sense of stage space, nor have they learned to 'draw figures and lines' with their bodies 'in stage space' (Chekhov 1928: 27). He identifies that actors have an impulse to use the space and that this manifests itself in the need to make the occasional expansive and expressive hand gesture, but Chekhov asks 'but why don't they want to make an expansive, fine and expressive gesture with their whole body?' (ibid.). He partly answers his own question by claiming that it is 'mimicry' that is at the root of the problem and that this destroys the body's expressiveness. Chekhov argues that this leads to the body becoming stiff and the gesture becoming reduced to a facial gesture, which, in itself, is insufficient on the stage. Furthermore, he claims that the actor's eyes only become fully expressive when the whole body is engaged.

EXILE

By 1927 **Stalin**'s clampdown on experiments in the arts was beginning and Chekhov was accused of being a mystic and a 'sick' actor who would spread corruption. Anthroposophy was banned in the Soviet Union and Chekhov was warned that he was about to be arrested. Therefore, he left Russia in 1928 and his work was discredited in the Soviet Union and not returned to the official curriculum until after 1969. This was

---

Joseph Stalin (1879–1953): a key figure in the Russian Revolution, Stalin became general secretary of the Communist Party in 1922. He became increasingly dictatorial after 1924. Debate was suppressed and artists had to conform to a particular kind of realism. The penalty for dissent was imprisonment or death.

Aleksandr Tairov (1885–1950): Russian director who created a dynamic and colourful physical theatre.

Formalism: an artistic movement which puts the emphasis on form rather than content. Opposed by the Soviet authorities after 1927 because it didn't pay enough attention to social content.

a period when the Soviet government was turning its attention towards theatre to ensure that it was serving the needs of the state and Meyerhold and another experimental theatre practitioner, **Aleksandr Tairov**, also came under attack. The fate of these three champions of non-naturalistic approaches to theatre indicates something of the dangers of failing to achieve government approval – Chekhov was forced into exile, never to return home; Tairov managed to make peace with the authorities and kept his theatre until his death in 1950; but Meyerhold, after numerous difficulties, was accused of **formalism** and stripped of his theatre in the early 1930s before being arrested and dying in custody in 1940. Meyerhold's actress wife, Zinaida Raikh, was murdered in their apartment by government agents.

WANDERING 1928–35

CHEKHOV AND MAX REINHARDT

Chekhov's first port of call when he left the Soviet Union was Berlin, where he hoped to stage *Hamlet*. Unfortunately he was unable to raise the funds and it was suggested to him that what audiences wanted was entertainment rather than serious drama. Disappointed, Chekhov accepted an invitation from the leading Austrian director, **Max Reinhardt**, who was at that time director of the Deutsches Theater in Berlin, to take the role of the clown, Skid, in the Vienna run of his production of Watters' and Hopkins' play, *Artists*, which had opened in Berlin on 9 June 1928. Although Reinhardt had a reputation as a director who welcomed and encouraged the creative input of his actors, Chekhov was working with his assistant, rather than with the great director himself, and wasn't very happy. Nonetheless, while *Artists* isn't considered one of Reinhardt's major productions and despite the fact that Chekhov's work on this play isn't even mentioned in a recent study of Reinhardt, Chekhov had an important experience during a performance of the play that affected his future thinking on the art of acting. During a monologue, Chekhov had a strong sense of being separate from the character. The character was in pain, but the actor, Chekhov, had a feeling of ease and calm. This sense of the separation between actor and character, where the actor doesn't have to fully feel the emotions of the character, had been discussed in the European theatre since the time of the French philosopher, **Denis Diderot**, whose

---

Max Reinhardt (1873–1943): Austrian director who was famous for huge theatrical spectacles which toured Europe. Made a film of *A Midsummer Night's Dream* in Hollywood (1935) and emigrated to the US in 1937 as the situation in Europe deteriorated.

Denis Diderot (1713–84): French writer and philosopher who argued that the actor must have a part of his consciousness which is always observing and making aesthetic judgements. The actor appears emotionally spontaneous and free but is, in fact, highly disciplined and controlled.

---

essay, 'The Actor's Paradox', was published posthumously in 1830. Stanislavsky's ideas of the actor using his own emotions as the character's appeared to go against this idea of dual consciousness. But Chekhov's experience in the role of Skid went beyond a simple return to Diderot's idea. Chekhov claims that he saw Skid from the outside, as if he were a member of the audience or one of his fellow actors, and that Skid was indicating to Chekhov how he should sit, move and speak (Gordon 1987: 148). This sense that the character exists outside of the actor is important. Chekhov used this event as further evidence for the existence of a higher ego.

Meeting Stanislavsky in Vienna soon after the performance in 1929, Chekhov insisted on the importance of the imagination and attacked Stanislavsky's emphasis on 'emotional recall' for being dangerous (Gordon 1987: 149). In a lecture during 1941 he repeated his attack and argued for the importance of a divided consciousness:

> When we are possessed by the part and almost kill our partners and break chairs, etc., then we are not free and it is not art but hysterics. At one time in Russia we thought that if we were acting we must forget everything else. Of course, it was wrong. Then some of our actors came to the point where they discovered that real acting was when we could act and be filled with feelings, and yet be able to make jokes with our partners – two consciousnesses.
>
> (Chekhov 1985: 102)

By the time Chekhov gave this lecture, however, Stanislavsky had already acknowledged the significance of the actor's dual consciousness in *An Actor Prepares* (1936). It is unlikely that Chekhov was unaware of Stanislavsky's book, especially as the publisher sent a copy of the pre-publication manuscript to Dorothy Elmhirst at Dartington Hall.

After his return to Berlin, Chekhov continued his studies in anthroposophy and accepted an invitation to direct Habima in *Twelfth Night*. Habima was a Hebrew-speaking theatre, founded in Moscow in 1918, which had received support and teaching from Stanislavsky and international acclaim for its production of *The Dybbuk*, directed by Vakhtangov in 1922. The company was now wandering around Europe before settling in Palestine in 1931. There was considerable mutual respect between Chekhov and Habima because of its connections with Vakhtangov. Chekhov was able to work in an intense rehearsal process with fully trained actors, and the success of the production as it toured Europe convinced Chekhov that there was an audience for his kind of theatre. The Chekhov/Habima *Twelfth Night* was shown in London in 1932, and **John Gielgud** judged both direction and acting as 'so extraordinarily inventive' (1937: 32)

FRANCE, LATVIA AND LITHUANIA

In 1931 Chekhov moved to Paris, where, together with Georgette Boner, a former student of Max Reinhardt, he set up another studio. However, Chekhov encountered a number of difficulties. He had hoped that he would find support for his work from the large Russian émigré community in Paris, but he was disappointed. He staged an adaptation of Tolstoy's fairy tale, *The Castle Awakens*, which is itself a literary reworking of a traditional tale, experimenting with eurythmy and other ideas from Steiner, but the production was a commercial failure. In 1932 and 1933 he worked at the state theatres in the still independent Latvia and Lithuania and directed a production of **Richard Wagner**'s *Parsifal*, also establishing a school in Riga. During a rehearsal of *Parsifal*, however, Chekhov, just into his forties, had his first heart attack. While he was still recovering, there was a fascist revolution in Latvia and he had to leave, travelling first to Italy and then back to France.

Chekhov was not the only practitioner, interested in dreams and with a vision of a new theatre, who was finding it hard to get support for his ideas in Paris at this time. The controversial French actor, director, writer and film-maker, **Antonin Artaud**, was struggling to get funding to set up his visionary Theatre of Cruelty. Artaud had worked with some of the key figures in French theatre and published his 'The Theatre of Cruelty: First Manifesto' in 1932 and the 'Second Manifesto' and his lecture 'Theatre and the Plague' in 1933. Like Chekhov, Artaud believed that the theatre had lost touch with its roots and that it shouldn't be seen as pure entertainment, but as a means to effect personal and social change. Artaud's personal difficulties were even more severe than Chekhov's. Addicted to laudanum rather than alcohol to ease his personal suffering, he was unable to find a means of coming to terms with his inner turbulence and spent most of the last ten years of his short life in psychiatric institutions. Artaud chose to focus on the dark aspect of dreams, believing that theatre should have a direct and violent impact. In fact, Artaud sounds, superficially at least, as if he is encouraging what Chekhov referred to as 'hysterics'. If Chekhov was aware of Artaud's work he makes no reference to it and, by the time Artaud's production of *The Cenci* was staged in 1935, Chekhov had left Paris.

Antonin Artaud (1896–1948): innovative French theatre practitioner who wanted to get away from psychological realism and develop a theatre which used sound, gesture and movement. His influential collection of essays, *The Theatre and its Double*, was published in 1938.

THE MOSCOW ARTS PLAYERS AND THE GROUP THEATRE

In 1935 Chekhov put together a company of exiled Russian actors for a short tour of the US with seven plays and an evening of stage adaptations of Anton Chekhov stories. The company, billed as the Moscow Arts Players, played in New York, Philadelphia and Boston. Chekhov also gave a lecture-demonstration to **The Group Theatre** at the invitation of the actress, **Stella Adler**. In this lecture-demonstration Chekhov suggested that, when approaching a character, the actor must first identify the archetype on which the character is based. He also outlined his theory of centres and the imaginary body and considered the notion of personal atmosphere (Gordon 1987: 155–9). The Group Theatre, which modelled itself on the MAT, had been founded in 1931 by Harold Clurman, Cheryl Crawford and **Lee Strasberg**. In 1934 the company found itself hosting a conflict between Strasberg, who placed his emphasis on the actor's emotional memory, and Adler, who had just returned from visiting Stanislavsky in Paris and put the emphasis on the method of physical actions that Stanislavsky was developing at the time. Her conflict with Strasberg continued until his death (and even beyond) and she emphasised the actor's use of the imagination – her teachings

The Group Theatre (1931–41): American company inspired by Stanislavsky and the MAT. The Group focused specifically on plays concerned with contemporary social issues by new American playwrights. The Group was founded by the director, teacher and critic, Harold Clurman (1901–80), Cheryl Crawford (1902–86), a superb organiser, and Lee Strasberg.

Stella Adler (1903–92): studied acting with Richard Boleslavsky and Maria Ouspenskaya in the 1920s and joined The Group Theatre in 1931. She established her own school, The Stella Adler Conservatory, in 1949.

Lee Strasberg (1901–82): acting teacher and director who studied with Boleslavsky and Ouspenskaya. A founder member of The Group Theatre, he taught a version of Stanislavsky's work which became known as 'the Method'. Strasberg's approach emphasised emotion-memory as the root of the actor's art.

suggest the impact of Chekhov as much as of Stanislavsky. Adler and Clurman were among those members of The Group Theatre who were impressed by Chekhov; particularly, by the combination of honesty and truth in his performance – which they associated with Stanislavsky's approach – together with a sense of rhythm, colour and design. Lee Strasberg, on the other hand, was among the unimpressed and suggested that Chekhov should be sent back to the Soviet Union – a strong remark given that Chekhov would have been imprisoned, if not executed, on his return. However, to be fair to Strasberg, not many people in the mid 1930s were aware of the plight of those artists who failed to win the approval of the state.

THE STUDIOS

DARTINGTON HALL 1935–8

It was while he was in New York that Chekhov met **Beatrice Straight** and **Deirdre Hurst du Prey**. Straight and Hurst du Prey were looking for someone to create a theatre course for the experimental community at **Dartington Hall** in Devon and Chekhov was recommended

Figure 1.1
Michael Chekhov as the Papa in
The Bridegroom and the Papa,
based on a story by Anton
Chekhov (*c.* 1931)

Figure 1.2

Michael Chekhov in *I Forgot*, based on a story by Anton Chekhov (*c.* 1932)

as a possibility. Greatly impressed by Chekhov, Straight contacted her mother, Dorothy Elmhirst, and said that this was the teacher they needed. Dorothy and her husband, Leonard, managed to travel to the US and see Chekhov perform in Philadelphia. Similarly impressed, they invited him to take up the post. Chekhov accepted the invitation and moved to England in October 1935. Given that du Prey claims that the only English Chekhov knew at this time was 'How do you do?', this was a huge gamble on both sides.

In April 1936 Chekhov began a series of classes with Deirdre Hurst du Prey and Beatrice Straight in order to train them as his assistants. This initial training lasted three months and comprised eighteen lessons. The first lesson was on concentration and Chekhov predicted that students would become bored and frustrated with work. Rather than trying to find something more 'interesting', however, the teacher must use her concentration to keep the students focused on the difficult tasks. As Chekhov put it:

> It is essential that they have difficult times and find things hard and not to their liking. They must learn to be students.

(du Prey 2000: 16)

Beatrice Straight (1914–2001): American actress and daughter of Dorothy Elmhirst from an earlier marriage. She was a talented actress and won an Oscar for her performance in the film *Network* (1975).

Deirdre Hurst du Prey (b. 1906): Canadian actress and assistant to Chekhov at both Dartington and Ridgefield, du Prey collected a vast amount of material relating to Chekhov's life and work.

Dartington Hall: Leonard Elmhirst (1893–1972) and Dorothy Whitney Elmhirst (1887–1968) bought the Dartington Estate in Devon, England, in 1925 and set up an experimental school. They were interested in how the arts could be used to transform both the individual and society.

This is a common experience – we begin to learn something new and are excited and full of enthusiasm, but as we continue in our studies we can feel that we're repeating the same things. Nothing seems new any more and we can't see the point of the repetition. The teacher's task is to help us to recognise that this is a phase we need to go through and to give encouragement. Chekhov wanted there to be a spirit of joy and lightness in the studio and he realised that his students would have to learn to overcome the dullness and heaviness that could easily dampen their work.

Chekhov had the reputation of being a very gentle teacher who challenged his students but did not torment them or overly criticise them, and some of this attitude he developed from his teachers, such as Leopold Sulerzhitsky. On the other hand, although he had a great deal of respect for Stanislavsky, Chekhov thought that he was a very poor teacher.

The Chekhov Theatre Studio opened with its first class at Dartington on 5 October 1936. There were twenty students, only four of them British, with twelve from the US and Canada. The fees for each student were £150 per year for tuition, food and accommodation. That British students were in a minority says quite a lot about the state of the theatre in Britain at this time, which was lagging behind developments in the rest of Europe. Gielgud, perhaps the leading English actor of his day, lamented the shortage of good schools for actors, but pointed hopefully towards Chekhov's Studio, as well as to Michel St Denis's London

Theatre School (Gielgud 1937: 32). The Chekhov Studio, then, was at the forefront of theatre training in Britain at the end of the 1930s. It is unfortunate that so few British actors were able to take advantage of the opportunity to study with him.

The arrangement at Dartington was ideal for Chekhov, because there were no commercial pressures and he was free to develop his system of training. Chekhov planned a three-year course, which would include the development of concentration and imagination, eurythmy, voice and speech (drawing on Steiner) and musical composition. Folk tales were to be studied, both as a means of freeing the imagination and as the key to understanding a culture, and students would start with short scenes and improvisations, gradually building to longer and more difficult pieces. After completing the three years' training the students would be eligible to join the school's touring company, which would provide them with their first professional experience. This direct link between training and professional practice demonstrates that Chekhov was always thinking of training in terms of its application within a professional context.

Dartington was an exciting place to be at this time, especially for those interested in developments in modern dance. The choreographer, Kurt Jooss (1901–79), famous for his anti-war piece, *The Green Table* (1932), had fled Germany with his company, the Ballets Jooss, and taken up residence at Dartington in 1934. Jooss's former teacher, Rudolf Laban (1879–1958), was exiled from Germany in 1938 and moved to Dartington, where he continued to investigate movement as a means of unifying the different art forms. The Indian modern dance pioneer, Uday Shankar (1900–77), also visited Dartington during this period. The possibilities for collaboration and cross-fertilisation were huge, but there was insufficient time for these possibilities to unfold.

Unfortunately, the school at Dartington wasn't to last three years because of the worsening situation in Europe. The Second World War didn't start until 1939, but the German occupation of Austria and parts of Czechoslovakia in 1938 and the ongoing Civil War in Spain signalled what was to come. Chekhov decided to move to the US with those who were able to accompany him. Beatrice Straight found an appropriate space at Ridgefield, Connecticut, and the new school opened there in December 1938.

RIDGEFIELD (1938–42)

By this time the main components of Chekhov's system were in place: 'imagination and concentration', 'higher ego', 'atmospheres and qualities', 'centres', 'imaginary bodies', 'radiance' and 'style'. Chekhov also added what came to be known as the 'four brothers', a series of linked exercises that focused on feelings of 'ease' (to replace Stanislavsky's 'relaxation'), 'form', 'beauty', and 'the whole'.

Unfortunately there was more financial pressure on Chekhov in Connecticut than there had been in Devon; the school had to be self-sufficient and students were charged fees of $1,200 per year. Chekhov attracted enough students to make the school a going concern and the curriculum was structured into five main areas of work: the technique of acting, training and developing the imagination, speech formation, eurythmy and dramatic studies that involved improvisations and scenes from plays. Both eurythmy and speech formation were based on the work of Rudolf Steiner. In a addition to this basic curriculum, students were each required to learn stage design, lighting, set building and make-up. Chekhov was interested in training theatre-artists who understood the complete process of theatre production in a practical way.

With less security at Ridgefield than he'd had at Dartington, although the Elmhirsts still continued their generous patronage, Chekhov was keen to get a production together and have his work seen

---

Fyodor Dostoevsky (1821–81): Russian novelist whose novels *Crime and Punishment* (1866) and *The Brothers Karamazov* (1880) are considered among the best ever written. Dostoevsky was imprisoned in a Siberian labour camp for five years for belonging to a socialist circle. His views on the world changed as a result of his experience and he came to believe that individual and social transformation was only possible through suffering and faith.

Yul Brynner (1920–85): actor who achieved international fame with his performance in the film of *The King and I* (1956). Born in Russia, Brynner worked as a circus performer in France before joining Chekhov in the US in 1941.

and acknowledged. He started work on *The Possessed*, which opened in New York in October 1939 and ran for a month. This production comprised fifteen scenes based on written episodes and recorded improvisations, in turn based on three novels by the outstanding Russian writer, **Fyodor Dostoevsky**. The production received significant praise for the quality of the ensemble work, the standard of the characterisation and the clarity of the speech. However, *The Possessed* wasn't as successful as Chekhov hoped it would be and he abandoned the plan to stage a production based on *The Pickwick Papers* by Charles Dickens. Instead, he organised a tour of Shakespeare's *Twelfth Night* and a short play based on Dickens' *The Cricket on the Hearth* to East Coast Universities in 1940. The tour was reasonably successful and not only met the aim of providing professional experience for those students selected, but also attracted new students to the school, including **Yul Brynner**. In 1941 the tour was expanded and included *King Lear* as well as *Twelfth Night* – the latter had a short run at the Little Theatre on Broadway in December that attracted a more generally positive response than had *The Possessed*. Shortly afterwards, in 1942, there was an evening of one-act adaptations of short stories by Anton Chekhov and there were criticisms that the students' performance lacked spontaneity.

It was during this period at Ridgefield that Chekhov began to formulate his ideas on the 'psychological gesture', which had been in the process of gestation since the 1920s.

THE HOLLYWOOD YEARS

Unfortunately, however, the attack by the Japanese on the American naval base at Pearl Harbor in 1941 precipitated the entry of the United States into the Second World War. By 1942 pressures on Chekhov's school were increasing, as rationing restricted the resources available for touring and as some of the male students were drafted into the forces. Chekhov closed the school and moved to Los Angeles in 1943, where he began a film career in Hollywood as well as teaching acting classes and giving lectures on acting and the creative process.

Chekhov made nine films in Hollywood and it was the third, *Spellbound*, which gained him the most recognition. *Spellbound*, released in 1945, was directed by **Alfred Hitchcock** and starred **Ingrid Bergman** and **Gregory Peck**, both of whom studied privately with

Sir Alfred Hitchcock (1899–1980): English director known as 'the master of suspense' and celebrated for films such as *Rear Window* (1954), *Vertigo* (1958), *North by Northwest* (1959) and *Psycho* (1960).

Ingrid Bergman (1925–82): Swedish film actress whose first Hollywood success was in *Casablanca* (1942).

Gregory Peck (1916–2003): American actor who appeared on Broadway with Stella Adler in a show directed by Max Reinhardt, before moving into films.

Chekhov. Peck plays John Ballantine, a man who is suffering from amnesia and has taken on the identity of a famous psychiatrist, Dr Edwardes. Once the false identity is discovered, Ballantine is suspected of murdering Edwardes and goes on the run, accompanied by Dr Constance Peterson (Ingrid Bergman), to try to discover the truth of what happened. Peterson takes Ballantine to her old mentor, played by Michael Chekhov, who, she hopes, will be able to analyse Ballantine's dreams and help him unlock his memory. Chekhov's role is a small one in terms of the amount of time he's on screen, but it's a pivotal role in the film. He gives a finely detailed performance as the old professor, which, although far from the great experimental performances of the 1920s as Erik XIV, Khlestakov and Hamlet,

Anthony Quinn (1915–2001): Mexican actor whose first film appearance was in 1936. His most famous film role was as Zorba in *Zorba the Greek* (1964).

Jack Palance (b. 1919): American film actor, perhaps best known for his 'bad guy' characterisations in movies from the 1950s.

Marilyn Monroe (1926–62): perhaps the most famous of all American film actresses, she studied with Lee Strasberg as well as attending classes with Chekhov.

Paul Rogers (b. 1917): English actor and student of Chekhov's at Dartington, Rogers has had a long and successful stage and screen career.

Hurd Hatfield (1917–98): American actor who studied with Chekhov at Dartington and Ridgefield. An extended career in film and television was perhaps overshadowed by an early success as the lead in the film adaptation of *The Picture of Dorian Gray* (1945).

demonstrates his humour and a precise control of physical actions. The quality of his work on this role earned him an Oscar nomination.

In 1946 Chekhov directed the Laboratory Theatre in *The Government Inspector*, but he was working as a guest director rather than as the director of students trained in his technique. After Ridgefield, Chekhov didn't establish another school or company and he didn't direct another production after *The Government Inspector*. He did, however, continue to lecture and teach acting classes in Hollywood. He often worked with already established Hollywood performers such as Ingrid Bergman, Gregory Peck, **Anthony Quinn**, **Jack Palance** and **Marilyn Monroe**. Monroe described Chekhov as 'the most brilliant man' she'd ever known and others also had immense respect for his teaching. We must be careful, however, not to attribute the success of these actors to their encounters with Chekhov. It is too easy to see a list of big names and then make assumptions about the effectiveness of his teaching. Chekhov's aim was art, not fame, and he was very aware that, in Hollywood and the commercial theatre, the two don't always go together. Several of those who studied with him for a significant period of time at Dartington, Ridgefield or Hollywood went on to have long and successful careers. **Paul Rogers**, **Hurd Hatfield** and Beatrice Straight have perhaps been the most successful of those from Dartington and Ridgefield. **Eddy Grove**, **Joanna Merlin**, **Mala Powers** and **Jack Colvin**, the latter three still active in promoting Chekhov's teaching, began to study with him during his time in Hollywood.

Chekhov's Hollywood career was interrupted by a heart-attack during the filming of *Arch of Triumph* in 1948 and ended after a second heart attack in 1954.

Eddy Grove (1917–95): American actor who studied with Chekhov in Hollywood and continued to teach the technique until just before his death.

Joanna Merlin: American actress and casting director who studied with Chekhov in Hollywood and continues to teach the Chekhov technique.

Mala Powers (b. 1931): American actress and executrix of the Chekhov estate. A member of Reinhardt's Junior Workshop in Hollywood, Powers' first film appearance was in 1942. Still active as a performer and a teacher of the Chekhov technique.

Jack Colvin: American film and TV actor who studied with Chekhov in Hollywood and continues to teach the Chekhov technique.

2

WRITINGS ON THE TECHNIQUE OF ACTING

INTRODUCTION

The publication of Michael Chekhov's *To the Actor* in 1953 was a landmark event in actor training. None of the other key figures of the first half of the twentieth century, including Stanislavsky, Meyerhold, Vakhtangov, **Brecht**, **Copeau**, **Saint-Denis**, Artaud and Craig, had produced a workbook for the actor. Stanislavsky's trilogy on actor training beginning with *An Actor Prepares* (1936), for example, presents his system through a story of a student's progress which includes a description of exercises, but these descriptions are part of the narrative rather than being an invitation to the reader to experiment on their own. Chekhov's book, in contrast, is not a story but a series of essays on key aspects of his method with exercises clearly marked out from the rest of the text to encourage the student to experiment. In an introductory note to his book Chekhov requests the reader's help, claiming that the contents of the book cannot be understood merely by reading, but only through practical application. While Chekhov acknowledges the importance of working with an experienced teacher, he also has a faith that working through the exercises in the book, on one's own or with a group, will be an effective means of developing an actor's skills.

To the Actor went through different versions. Chekhov started the first English version of the book in 1937 at Dartington and finished it in 1942, but it was rejected by publishers. Chekhov felt that his written

Bertolt Brecht (1898–1956): brilliant German playwright and massively influential, if frequently misunderstood, theorist. Brecht's views on acting are often set against those of Stanislavsky, because he didn't want the actor to become identified with the character. New York productions of *A Threepenny Opera* in 1933 and *The Mother* in 1935 were poorly received by the critics. Brecht himself moved to the US in 1941 and, like Chekhov, was based in Hollywood until the end of the war.

Jacques Copeau (1879–1949): French director, actor and theorist. He had a major influence on French twentieth-century theatre and on the development of mime and physical theatre.

Michel Saint-Denis (1897–1971): French actor, director, teacher and nephew of Copeau, Saint-Denis moved to England in 1935 to direct and establish a theatre school. He also set up schools in France and the US.

English was to blame and translated the work into Russian, publishing it privately in 1945 and sending copies to the libraries of American universities with Russian departments. He then re-translated the work into English only to suffer rejection once again. In 1952, Chekhov gave Charles Leonard permission to edit the manuscript in any way he saw fit and Leonard's reduced version of *To the Actor* was published in English in 1953. It is in Leonard's version that Chekhov's work became widely known. In 1991 Mala Powers, ex-student of Chekhov and executrix of the Chekhov estate, re-edited the 1942 manuscript in collaboration with Mel Gordon and it was published by HarperCollins as *On the Technique of Acting*. This version claimed to be the 'first complete edition' of *To the Actor* but, while it contains material absent from the 1953 version, it also leaves out material. In this way neither edition can be said to be complete. The arrangement of the material within each book is also significantly different and it's not possible to create a 'complete' version just by including the missing sections. Both versions offer a description of the key elements of the Chekhov technique together with exercises to enable the reader to test the theory in practice. Perhaps the major difference between the two versions is in the number of exercises included: there are eighty-seven in *On the Technique of Acting*, compared to only seventeen in the earlier version, although the difference is partly owing to the way in which exercises are broken into different stages. There are, however, over a hundred exercises published in total and many more included in the unpublished records of Chekhov's classes.

In 2002 a new edition of *To the Actor* was published which includes the whole text of the 1953 edition plus additional material not previously available in English. The next section follows the structure of *On the Technique of Acting* as it was the most readily available edition of the book at the time of writing. I make reference to both versions of the book as well as to some of Chekhov's other writings in order to bring out some points more clearly.

IMAGINATION AND CONCENTRATION

Chekhov wants to draw our attention to the fact that images appear to us without our consciously willing them. The obvious time when images appear without our control is when we are asleep. Have you ever wondered about how dreams are so convincing, even though they're not always realistic? They conform to their own rules of composition and 'impossible' events happen, yet we can be fully absorbed in them and our emotions are involved. Sometimes, of course, we have another layer of awareness and know in the dream that we are asleep and dreaming. Before we fall asleep, however, there are often a few moments when we're between waking and sleeping and images and sounds of what's happened during the day appear, sometimes merging into each other or transforming; and sometimes we have the feeling of having understood something that we hadn't noticed before. As we follow the images we may move further away from our memories of the day and enter into an experience that takes our raw material and weaves it into imaginary landscapes and figures. These images and sounds are known as 'hypnagogic phenomena' and the state in between waking and sleep is called 'hypnagogia'. Not everyone is aware of these phenomena in the same way that not everyone remembers their dreams – but we all dream.

DREAMING AS A CREATIVE PROCESS

Dreams interested Chekhov because they are an example of a creative process that is independent of our everyday identity. In his reaction against Stanislavsky, Chekhov was looking for a way of enabling the actor to go beyond personal memories, and he felt that dreams were an example of creativity which wasn't personal. This is also true of hypnagogic phenomena, but there is an important difference for Chekhov between these and dreams. In hypnagogia we are still partly awake and Chekhov didn't want the actor to be a slave to the images that appeared, but to be able to enter into a dialogue with them. The task for the actor is not just to be carried along into dreamland, but to find a way of bringing these images into performance.

Ordinarily we might think of dreams and hypnagogic phenomena, if we think about them at all, as being very personal indeed – something that happens in our inner world that has very little relation to other people. Chekhov's claim that these experiences are a way of going beyond ourselves to make contact with an 'objective world of imagina-tion' (Chekhov 1991: 3) sounds odd if we believe that our dreams and our imaginings are 'subjective' and therefore not really of much signifi-cance, except, perhaps, for ourselves.

Chekhov has no interest in analysing dreams to find out what their hidden significance is – he treats the dream image as itself, as an inde-pendent being. When we dream we have the experience of being in a dream, but when we wake up and remember we believe that the dream was in us. Chekhov wants us to consider that dreams, hypnagogic phenomena and other products of the imagination come from outside of us. If we can imagine this, if we can behave as if these images are independent of us, then we have the possibility of not reducing them to ourselves and our own personal concerns, but of expanding to find out more about them.

BEYOND THE PLAYWRIGHT

This idea is then applied to characters within plays, for example the plays of Shakespeare. Hamlet is not a real person but a product of the imagination, yet, for Chekhov, he exists apart from Shakespeare's text. Chekhov imagines Shakespeare watching his characters with his 'creative gaze' and engaging with them to find out more about them and seeing how they interact with other characters. Whether or not Shakespeare actually did this, or even thought about whether or not he was doing it, we don't really know. The truth or otherwise of this doesn't really matter; Shakespeare is used as an example of how we might develop a dialogue with the characters that we encounter through our imagination. When Shakespeare wrote the character of Hamlet he didn't exhaust everything that could be said of the character; there is always more to be found and it is the actor's task to find out more than Shakespeare wrote. What does Chekhov mean by this? On a simple level, whatever we can say of something doesn't exhaust our experience of it. We often have the experience of sensing more about a person, object or event than we can put into words. How often, when asked what we thought about a performance we've enjoyed, do we find ourselves struggling for words? Whatever we say just doesn't seem to be enough; there is always something left over. The listener has to use their imagination to get a sense of the event and will inevitably fill in missing details. These added bits, however, aren't necessarily what was in the speaker's mind. Let's try a little example:

Sam walked along the hot dusty road.

What do you see when you imagine this? Is Sam male or female, for example? Dark or light skinned? What about the clothes? The style of walking? What expression is on the face? What are the arms doing? How fast is Sam moving? Is it a slow walk or a quick walk? How about going into more detail? What, if anything, is the little finger of Sam's left hand doing? Is the weight evenly balanced on each foot? And how about the road? Is it busy? Quiet? What time of day is it? What country is it? The trick here is to get the answer from the image, which means using language slightly differently. Rather than ask the question 'How is Sam walking?', Chekhov would address the question to Sam as in 'Sam, can you show me how you're walking along the hot dusty road?'. Try this and see if you can sense a different quality in your relationship to the image. If you can, what is the difference?

The questions we can ask are potentially infinite and each answer we get adds a little more to the image. But we will probably get very different responses to the questions. Each of us will get a different image of Sam walking along the road. Of course, if we are learning a play we will have considerably more information about our character. Gender and race might be clearly defined and there will be all kinds of qualities we discover about the character through what they say and do and how they relate to others, but there will always be something left over no matter how detailed the playwright's description. It is in these gaps that the actor's imagination comes to the fore, and that Chekhov sees the opening for the actor's creativity to flourish. Some playwrights leave more space than others and a group of actors devising their own material have the most space of all.

NOT ME BUT THE CHARACTER . . .

Once you had done the exercise above it might have come as a surprise to you that Sam could have been either male or female. Throw away your first image and do the exercise again, this time allowing for the possibility that the figure might be of either sex. What are the differences between your first image and your second? Chekhov advises discarding your first image. You can always go back to it if it feels that it was the most appropriate one for the task, but it is a mistake to be satisfied with the first image that emerges and go no further. The quest is for the richest image, the one that contains the most information about the character. This is one way of avoiding cliché and repeating old habits. A key idea here is that the character is different from you and has a different body, a different psychology and a different way of moving. Chekhov deals later on with how the actor embodies these differences, but for the moment it is sufficient to note the importance of this difference. To see the character as other than ourselves is to make a fundamentally different move from the Stanislavskian approach. The aim of an actor trained in the Chekhov technique is not 'How would *I* behave if I were in this situation?' but 'How does the *character* behave in these circumstances?'. It might be the case that we would behave in the same way as the character – that is perfectly possible – but the first question must be about the character's behaviour, not our own. The result might be that the character's behaviour is so greatly different from our own that we find it difficult to embody. That is really at the heart of the technique – *how to develop the skills to transform ourselves into a character who looks and behaves in ways that are very different from ourselves.*

There is more to Chekhov's use of the imagination than just seeing the outer behaviour of the character. Chekhov wants us to get a sense of the character's psyche through our imagination. To return to the example, we might ask what Sam is thinking or feeling while walking along the road; those would be questions relevant to the specific moment. But there is still another level of engagement, which is not *what* Sam's thinking or feeling, but *how*. What makes the way Sam thinks about a subject different from 'how' you think about it. This how will need to be manifest in stage behaviour for the audience to understand, but the point to grasp at the moment is that it is important to recognise that people have different styles of thinking and feeling. This is partly what we mean by character. Furthermore, this difference might be an imaginative one that is not based on the observation of real-life people. Differentiating his work from Stanislavsky's 'true-to-life' approach, Chekhov asked 'what if the character's psychology and inner life are *not* true to life? Was Don Quixote true to life?' (Leonard 1984: 38).

NOT NATURE BUT ART

How to embody the character comes later. In this section Chekhov is concerned with opening the reader up to the world of images and encouraging the development of an aesthetic awareness. If the actor is to be an artist – and Chekhov, like Stanislavsky, Craig and Copeau, among others, thought that this was important – then a sense of what is artistically appropriate needs to be developed. Not just anything is good enough to be placed onstage before an audience. Chekhov wants the actor to be able to feel what's right and he calls this a 'sense of truth' and suggests that the way to develop this sense is through an engagement with great works of the past – not just theatre works, but also painting, architecture, sculpture, music and literature. You might also want to add film, video, photography and computer graphics. What's important for Chekhov is that we develop an understanding of composition, of how things are put together and what happens to the whole when one or more elements are altered.

DEVELOPING AN ARTISTIC AWARENESS

The first exercise offered in *On the Technique of Acting* involves a study of architectural forms. Chekhov claims that it is sufficient to work from pictures and that it isn't necessary to be studying specialised books on architecture. What's required is that we look at the images of the buildings and try to get a sense of line, form, dimensions and weight. The first stage is to get a sense of the whole and then the relationship of the parts to the whole. Chekhov suggests that we try to 'guess' the function of the various parts – are they there to support, decorate or protect? The question is: What is this part for? It's possible to explore framing the question as if you are 'asking' the part itself, in the same way that it was suggested that you can ask the character to show you how they move. Asking a part of a building a question about its function might seem a little odd, even odder than asking an imaginary character, but it is another way to approach the imagination and to develop an artistic intuition. Once you feel that you have a good sense of the whole and of the function of the parts, the next task is to vary imaginatively the proportions and dimensions of the parts. How would it be if the windows were smaller or larger, for example? Or if the roof shape changed? What if the building was constructed out of a different material? This kind of exploration can also be done with painting and sculpture, for example by varying the shapes and colours. It could also be done with music and we might consider not only the melodic line, rhythm and tempo, but also instrumentation. Working in this way assists us both to appreciate the original and to free up our own creativity.

A SENSE OF THE WHOLE

When this exercise is applied to a play we need to get a sense of the whole and then develop an awareness of how the various parts contribute to the effect of that whole. One way in which we can develop this is by considering the story and the plot of the play and varying the different elements. This can be done in different ways. How would it be, for example, if the scene order was altered? How would this affect the play as a whole? What would happen if characters behaved or felt differently?

Consider how this might be a useful approach in practice, either in the process of rehearsing a script or in working on a devised piece. If we're working on a pre-existent script, it can be helpful to get a sense of the things that don't happen. In what follows I'm going to refer to two Shakespeare plays, but you can choose any plays you like to perform the same exercise. For example, in Act 3 Scene 3 of *Hamlet*, King Claudius is at prayer and Hamlet contemplates killing him at that moment, but decides against it. What would have happened if Claudius had been killed at that point? What would happen next? How would it affect our feelings for Hamlet? Or Claudius? What would happen to

Figure 2.1 Michael Chekhov teaching in the studio at Dartington

the relationship between Hamlet and Ophelia? This is an important moment in the play and, if we allow Hamlet to kill Claudius, we would have to make major changes to what comes next. Or think of *Romeo and Juliet*. In Act 3 Scene 1 Romeo fights and kills Tybalt. What would have happened if Tybalt had killed Romeo? Or if Romeo had taken another course of action? If Romeo doesn't kill Tybalt, then he doesn't need to go into exile and the chain of circumstances that leads to the lovers' deaths is broken.

Contrast this with a change which Baz Luhrmann makes in his film version of *Romeo and Juliet* (1996) with Leonardo DiCaprio and Claire Danes. Luhrmann's film is full of imaginative and effective changes to the original text, but there is one particular change which I want to focus on. In Act 5 Scene 3 of Shakespeare's text Paris sees Romeo entering the tomb and tries to arrest him (remember Romeo is wanted for the slaying of Tybalt). The two fight and Romeo kills Paris. In Luhrmann's film this fight and Paris's death are cut. This omission makes no difference to what happens next. On the other hand it would make a huge difference if Paris were to kill Romeo, or even just to arrest him successfully. What function do you think the fight between Paris and Romeo serves in Shakespeare's text? Take a look at Luhrmann's film – does he find another way of fulfilling this function? Does the removal of this killing alter the way in which we feel about Romeo?

These questions help us to understand the way a performance works. In Luhrmann's film, Juliet begins to wake up and move her hand before Romeo takes the poison. As spectators we are invited to imagine what would happen if Romeo noticed. It's the kind of moment that might make us want to cry out to try and influence the action. This is a very small action but a very powerful one. Too big and we won't believe that Romeo didn't notice, too small and we may not notice. The moment isn't written into Shakespeare's script (very few stage directions are) but is a very good example of an imaginative addition which intensifies the intended mood of the original text. I have no idea how this moment was arrived at in the film. It might have been part of Luhrmann's shooting script, something he always planned, or it might have arisen during the shooting itself as a suggestion from one of the actors. It's not important what happened in this specific situation. The point is that it shows the kind of result that could have arisen from Chekhov's process of imaginative variation.

When we're working without a script, there is so much more possibility of variation and there is not necessarily a 'whole' at the beginning to get a grasp of. If we're devising from a pre-existent story there will be a whole, but if we're starting out from scratch then it is more difficult. Nonetheless, wherever we start from we have the possibility of trying different variations, either in our imaginations or in practice. The question to ask ourselves is which variation helps us best achieve what we're after, and this is true whether we're trying to generate specific meanings or create a piece where form is more important than content. This is a key question: 'Does this achieve what we're setting out to achieve?' – we'll return to it later.

FOLK TALES

Chekhov believed that folk tales provided the 'best material' for developing a sense of artistic truth. In fact Chekhov felt that these tales were so effective that it wasn't necessary to ask questions, because the tales would work in our 'creative subconscious' and 'implant' the sense of truth. Folk tales were, and still are, a very important source of material for those artists wishing to work in a non-naturalistic manner, but it is unclear why Chekhov considers it inappropriate to ask questions in the same way as with plays. Nor is it clear why Shakespeare's plays, for example, won't similarly work in our creative subconscious to imbue a sense of truth. It might be that folk tales are quite simple and the form is easily recognised and absorbed, but Chekhov appears to believe that folk tales are more truthful than plays. This is too complex a problem to go into in this book, but it is important to note that Chekhov is not alone in assigning a high value to folk tales and that there are literally hundreds of books which use folk tales as a way of helping us to better understand ourselves and our psychological processes.

Leaving aside the question of the relative value of folk tales, we can identify two ways of working with the imagination. One is to proceed by asking questions and making imaginative variations, and the other is to allow the material to sink into our subconscious and be transformed. In general, both of the approaches can be used to develop our imagination.

Involved in the training of the imagination is an awareness of the 'flexibility of images'. By imagining fairy-tale or dreamlike transformations (a frog into a prince, a flamingo into an elephant) and paying close attention to the stages of the transformation, we will develop both concentration and a facility for working with images.

CONCENTRATION

Concentration is very important in working with our imagination and, while Chekhov acknowledges that we all possess the power of concentration to some degree, noting that we wouldn't be able to cross the road without it, he claims that the actor needs to have a higher level of concentration than average. In his Lessons for Teachers, which were given at Dartington in 1936, Chekhov distinguishes between two kinds of concentration. The first is where something attracts our attention and holds it. This is an unwilled concentration which just happens – this is often our favourite kind because we don't have to do anything to get there but we are pleasantly absorbed. The second kind of concentration is a willed one and Chekhov gives the example of focusing on something which is unpleasant to us. Because this thing is unpleasant we don't want to concentrate on it, whatever it is, and we have to make a conscious effort to concentrate – we have to overcome an inner resistance. Often we don't want to learn new things because they're difficult, or we don't want to repeat exercises every day because we feel they become boring, giving us an attitude of 'I've done all of this before.' In those moments we're not concentrated on the task, but distracted, and this prevents us from deepening our awareness of our work. Yet, although we may need to overcome an inner resistance, Chekhov doesn't want us to force ourselves or to bully ourselves into working. A sense of ease is important for Chekhov in everything that we do and we need to bring our attention gently to the task at hand, ensuring that we are not tense in any way. Concentration doesn't mean furrowing our brow and trying to convince people that we're 'trying hard'; it means an ability to bring our attention to an object inside or outside of ourselves and to hold it there without excess tension. Without the ability to concentrate our attention wanders. Chekhov's exercises in concentration are designed to enable us to train our attention, so that we notice when we become distracted and are able to bring our minds back to the task at hand. Clearly this requires practice, but this is true of all aspects of any technical training; if we don't practice we won't improve.

If we can't concentrate then we can't effectively interact with our imagination and this will make our task of seeing the character in as much detail as possible very difficult indeed. An ability to concentrate is not just important for working with character – we need it to have a sense of the whole play and the flow of the performance; we need it to be able to keep our attention on our task in front of an audience and to be able to adapt to the changes in the performances of our colleagues; and we need it in order to train ourselves in the other aspects of the technique. The concentrated attention of the actors on the objects in the space, on each other and on the performance itself enables the audience to concentrate on the action being performed for them.

Work with imagination, concentration, relaxation and the development of a sense of truth are all aspects of the training that Chekhov received with Stanislavsky at the Moscow Arts Theatre. Chekhov developed in his own direction from these basic building blocks, devised new exercises and placed a different emphasis on different aspects. Dropped from Chekhov's approach are the exercises in affective or emotion memory, in which the actor draws on memories of past experiences in order to find out how they relate to the character's situation. Chekhov believed that this made art too personal. This isn't to say that our personal memories and experiences aren't an important part of our work as creative artists – they clearly are – but Chekhov prefers to approach them in a different way, as will become clear. Another changed emphasis is really a change in terminology for practical reasons. Rather than use the term 'relaxation' as Stanislavsky did, Chekhov referred to a 'feeling of ease', as he felt that this was a more accurate description of what was required.

How does this image of a dream work in relation to the theatre? When we view the character from the perspective of our higher ego, we see it within the context of the whole play. We are seeing both from the perspective of the character and from the perspective of a creative artist. This perspective can assist us to feel 'apart from' or 'above' the material we are working with, which is our own body. At the same time, however, the actor must be able to embody the images and, in addition to a well-developed and flexible imagination, Chekhov required the actor to have a body which was sensitive to inner impulses, noting that 'every actor, to a greater or lesser degree, suffers from some of [the] body's resistance' (2002: 2). Chekhov proposes a number of useful exercises for increasing the body's flexibility and responsiveness, but he notes that the exercises in concentration, atmosphere and imagination also assist in this process of sensitisation.

THE HIGHER EGO

Chekhov distinguished between our everyday personality or 'lower ego' and our 'higher ego', which he described as 'the artist in us that stands behind all our creative processes' (1991: 16). If we think about our experience of dreams for a moment, we can get a sense of what Chekhov means by this. When we dream we find ourselves in all kinds of situations, meeting different people – some we recognise from our waking lives and others are completely unknown to us. We have a sense of self in the dream; that is, there is a dream figure which each person identifies as 'me'. But while we have a sense of this everyday self as being 'in' a dream, there is also the part of us that is dreaming the whole situation. We are both a character in a dream and the creator of the dream. When we are awake and reflect on this it appears obvious, but when we are in the dream we are often unaware that we are also the dream creator. It is this dream creator which Chekhov sees as our higher ego and our task is to become aware of this aspect of ourselves when we are awake. From this point of view we might regard artistic activity as 'dreaming while awake'. The image of the dream also gives us the sense that the dreamer is a more expansive sense of self than the identity within the dream – more than our 'everyday' personality.

CREATIVE INDIVIDUALITY AND THE EVERYDAY SELF

In the 1953 version of *To the Actor*, Chekhov's thoughts on creative individuality and the everyday self are explained more clearly than in *On The Technique of Acting*. He makes a clear distinction between how we are in 'normal existence' and how we are in moments of creative 'inspiration':

In everyday life we identify ourselves as 'I'; we are the protagonists of 'I wish, I feel, I think.' This 'I' we associate with our body, habits, mode of life, family, social standing and everything else that comprises normal existence. But in moments of inspiration the *I* of an artist undergoes a kind of metamorphosis.

(2002: 86)

What exactly is the metamorphosis that Chekhov refers to here? He refers to an 'influx of power' (ibid.), which connects actor and audience. This sense of power involves a feeling of energy filling the stage and flowing into the auditorium and is a feeling of being fully present on the stage. When the actor experiences this energy Chekhov suggests that there is contact with the higher ego; instead of identifying with our everyday self we begin to identify with the creative self. It's quite difficult to get a sense of this experience if we've never had it, but we can begin to imagine what it might be like. How would it be if you were a fully creative person? How might you use your voice, emotions and actions to create a character? Can you see yourself in your mind's eye? Can you get a sense of distance between you as the creator and shaper of this character and the materials you are using; that is, your voice, emotions and actions? This is slightly different from the exercise above, in which you imagined Sam walking down the road – then you were imagining Sam as someone separate from you, now you are imagining yourself being transformed into someone else. An important difference between an actor and a painter or sculptor is that the material used to create the work of art, paint and canvas or stone, for example, is separate from the artist, whereas the actor's material isn't. Often we are too close to ourselves to notice our habitual actions and behaviours and, even if we do notice them, we may be too identified with them to want to change. From this perspective, how could we possibly view our voices, emotions and our bodies as raw material to be moulded? Wouldn't that mean changing who we are? But, if we can manage to create an internal distance, we add another dimension to the picture and we begin to see that what we identify with is only a part of ourselves, and that we can let go of our habitual actions and reactions in order to transform ourselves into a character. We can always return to our ordinary ways of doing things, but we will inevitably have a view of ourselves as being more flexible than we were, and this new flexibility has an effect on our daily life as well as on our creative life. In fact, we might begin to see to what extent we are creating our everyday lives.

PROBLEMS WITH THE HIGHER EGO

One problem for Chekhov is that the higher ego creates without respecting artistic boundaries. We can begin having too much fun with the transformations and even forget that the production we're in has a particular style and aim. The task of the everyday personality is to keep the higher ego focused on the task at hand, and to keep in touch with the reality of working on a theatrical production with other people, each of whom has their own higher ego. Another way of looking at it is that the 'power of inspiration always exceeds the power of expression' (Chekhov 2002: 88).

THE FOUR FUNCTIONS OF THE HIGHER EGO

Creative individuality

The higher ego is the source of what Chekhov called our 'creative individuality', that part of us which leads to us doing things differently from each other. For example, he suggests that we consider a group of painters attempting to paint, as accurately as possible, the same landscape. None of the pictures will be identical with another; each painter has a different way of responding to the landscape and what determines this way of responding is, according to Chekhov, the creative individuality of each artist. This is why no two interpretations of Hamlet or Juliet are the same – performers bring their own creative individuality to each role. No matter how well they get away from their everyday personality and transform themselves into the character, no two actors will play the same role in an identical manner. Chekhov suggests that we imagine the same part played by different actors whose work we know well and try to grasp the different ways in which each performer works. Then we should go on to imagine ourselves in the same role and get a sense of how our own creative individuality would lead us to perform the part. It is our creative individuality that enables each of us to go beyond what is literally there in front of us in the playwright's text in order to 'flesh out' the character.

Discerning the conflict between good and evil

For Chekhov the conflict between good and evil was central to the art of the theatre and the failure to recognise this ethical dimension would leave the performance flat. This conflict, however, is never between the 'purely good' and the 'purely evil', as this itself would lead to a flat performance. The actor's task is to find the ways in which different characters have both positive and negative qualities and to bring them into the performance.

The higher ego enables us to take a more multidimensional view of the various characters, seeing the complex intermixing of good and evil, rather than a one-dimensional view of 'goodies' and 'baddies'. When Shakespeare has Romeo kill Paris as he enters Juliet's tomb, we are forced to consider the ethical complexity of the situation. We can understand Romeo's desperation, but killing Paris is hardly something that we can view in a positive light. Paris has not been involved in the bloodshed between the Capulets and Montagues and he takes the 'official' view that Romeo's slaying of Tybalt was murder. If we think back to that moment, we can identify with Romeo's attempts to avoid conflict and with his revengeful rage, leading to fatal retaliation, when Tybalt has killed Mercutio. But we are also aware that Romeo's action is ultimately wrong and the killing of Paris emphasises this negative aspect of Romeo's character. When Baz Luhrmann cuts the death of Paris from his film version, the complexity produced by the interplay of the positive and negative qualities in Romeo's character is reduced. However sad Luhrmann's ending, there is the danger that it leads us into a sentimentality that negates our awareness of the fact that Romeo is a killer sentenced to death. The exclusion of the slaying of Paris leaves Romeo only with the 'understandable' killing of Tybalt to stain his character and therefore flattens out both the role and the audience response to it. Chekhov believed that it was the task of our higher ego to be able to encompass these ethical complexities and to make them relevant to our time. A question to ask of Luhrmann's film might be 'What does this representation of Romeo have to tell us about our current society?'. What do you think?

Developing a sensitivity to the audience

An awareness of how the specific ethical problems embedded within a play have relevance to a contemporary audience is also something which Chekhov considered to be the function of our higher ego. Chekhov contrasts the approach of Vakhtangov, who kept the audience in mind from the very first rehearsal, with an unnamed playwright who becomes so involved with reading his own play that he is unable to communicate with the audience. Chekhov sums up the difference quite brutally:

'Vakhtangov created for the audience, the playwright for himself' (1991: 22). The idea of understanding the audience and keeping it in mind while making a performance does not mean just trying to make productions in order to please the audience. It might be that we want to challenge the audience – to question their prejudices – but we have to know what these are before we can confront them. But it is not enough just to imagine that we know; we must go out and study current opinion through reading newspapers and paying attention to television, radio, cinema, theatre and the Web, as well as to our personal experience both inside and outside of the theatre.

Developing detachment, compassion and humour

The fourth function of the higher ego is the development of humour through the process of detachment. The higher ego 'frees us from ourselves' by enabling us to create a distance from our habitual identifications and be able to see them in a humorous light. We can then begin to see ourselves more objectively and take a more compassionate view of ourselves and of others. One of my students, when asked what she wanted from a course in improvisation, answered 'To get over myself' – this is precisely what Chekhov considers the higher ego will help us to do.

Put simply, what Chekhov calls our higher ego is our ability to detach from our habitual self-centredness and to see ourselves and the world in a more objective manner. This is not only beneficial for us as actors, but also in our everyday lives, and enables us to function with a lighter touch that is aware of the other person's position and the ethics of the situation.

OBJECTIVE ATMOSPHERE AND INDIVIDUAL FEELINGS

ATMOSPHERE

In everyday conversation we speak of places or events or relationships between people as having particular 'atmospheres'. We might simply say that there was a 'bad' or a 'good' atmosphere and the listener will have some sense of what we mean. It's not unusual for us to be even more discriminating, referring to atmospheres as peaceful, joyful, weird, heavy, light, miserable, bright, magical, etc. It is something that we sense as being 'in the air', rather than belonging to any particular person. Indeed an individual's particular feelings might be at odds with the general atmosphere. Can you imagine a party which has a wonderful, warm and joyful atmosphere, but where there is a person who is upset? – someone who is quietly crying because they're feeling alone and unloved while everyone else is having a good time? Perhaps the person feels even worse because they're aware of the joyful party atmosphere and feel at odds with it. This person isn't outside the atmosphere, but is feeling sad within the joyful atmosphere of the party. Both 'impersonal' atmosphere and personal feelings exist at the same time and in the same 'space'. A sensitivity to atmospheres and the ability to create them onstage is central to the work of Michael Chekhov, and he describes atmosphere as the 'soul' or the 'heart' of the performance – it is the feeling dimension which links everything together and forges a connection between actor and audience.

Atmosphere as process

Although theatre practitioners in Russia and elsewhere had discussed the importance of atmosphere from the beginning of the twentieth century, Chekhov developed the idea in theory and practice further than anyone else and it became one of the major elements in his technique. In order to develop our understanding of atmosphere, we need to be able to recognise the atmospheres that exist around us and notice their effect on our feelings. We also need become aware of the effect of our behaviour on these atmospheres – of when our personal atmosphere is strong enough to change the atmosphere around us. We don't see atmospheres any more than we see the air or the wind, but we feel them and they affect how we behave. We can notice the ways in which people are moved by specific atmospheres in the way that we can see leaves moved in the breeze and, as no two objects are affected in the same way by a gust of wind but respond according to their own natures, so different people are affected differently by the same atmosphere. Chekhov doesn't regard an atmosphere as something static, however, but as a process, something which is continually in motion and developing and which moves and inspires the actor who is open and responsive to it.

An experiment with atmosphere

Take a few moments to imagine being in a library. What kind of atmosphere does it have? How is this atmosphere different from an exciting party, or a place of worship, or a theatre, or a hospital ward? As you make these comparisons you will be imagining, however briefly, the atmospheres of these different places. Return to the library in your imagination and allow your sense of the atmosphere to develop; imagine moving in this atmosphere and the effect that it has on the way that you're feeling. How would you speak in this atmosphere? What would be the tone of your voice? If you feel like moving and speaking in this way, go ahead and explore (no one's looking!). Notice what feelings and thoughts emerge in response to the atmosphere. The idea isn't to try to force yourself to feel anything in particular, just to allow yourself to become aware of feelings that emerge in response to the atmosphere. Your experience might be very subtle; watch out for the critical part of yourself that might say to you that what you're experiencing isn't really significant, or that you're doing it wrong – Chekhov regards this part of ourselves as the enemy of the higher ego.

Now imagine that, still in the library, you can hear a group of noisy people outside. Perhaps they're drunk and happy, or having an argument. Imagine the group getting closer and eventually entering the library. What happens when they enter? Does their behaviour change? Do they quieten down? If, as a group, they entered the library with a noisy and aggressive atmosphere, then either the atmosphere of the library would change or the atmosphere of the group would. Chekhov argued that no two 'objective' atmospheres could exist for long in the same place because one would eventually prove stronger. These examples are 'objective' atmospheres because they don't belong to an individual: one is the atmosphere of the place and the other the atmosphere of the group.

You can also return to the other places and imagine their atmospheres and how you would speak and move; or think of the atmosphere of a beach on a summer's day, or your street on a moonlit night, or the atmosphere of a room where two people have been arguing. And you can imagine different people in these atmospheres and how they move and speak.

Once you've got the idea, you'll see that we're continually surrounded by atmospheres. Chekhov considered that there was no such thing as empty space, because places always have specific atmospheres. The place where we are going to give our performance is not empty of atmosphere, but has a distinct atmosphere of its own. This atmosphere might support that of the piece we're going to put on or it might not; if it does, then we must be aware of this and do our best to make our performance work in harmony with this atmosphere of place. On the other hand, if the place has an atmosphere which doesn't support our piece, we must ensure that we are able continually to transform the atmosphere for the duration of the performance.

Atmosphere as dominant tone

An atmosphere can be considered as the dominant tone or mood of, among other things, a place, an event, a relationship or a performance. An old ruined castle, for example, has a different atmosphere from a busy casualty department and each atmosphere will vary at specific times and have different effects on individuals in contact with them. Our first task is to become sensitive to the atmospheres around us; each place will have its own atmosphere. At the same time we need to become aware of how these atmospheres affect us.

Chekhov used the example of walking along and arriving at the crowded scene of a street accident; we will be aware of the atmosphere before we realise exactly what has happened. A sign that we have become aware of this atmosphere might be that we ask ourselves 'What's going on here?', or we might notice a physical sensation, such as our heart beating faster or our skin prickling. The moment these shifts in our experience occur we can notice that the atmosphere has caught us. Each individual in the scene will have their own response to the situation, but there will be a dominant atmosphere which is experienced as a whole and as external. That is, the atmosphere cannot be reduced to the experience of any single person, but has a life of its own which draws other people into it. In this sense Chekhov considered atmospheres to be 'objective'.

There is always a dominant atmosphere and, according to Chekhov, two objective atmospheres cannot coexist for long in the same space; one must always become dominant. In this example we might also notice how the accident has changed the atmosphere of the place. There is no such thing as an 'empty space' for Chekhov, because space is always filled with atmosphere. The place where the accident has taken place will have had an atmosphere prior to the event. Perhaps it had a very peaceful atmosphere, but the atmosphere of the accident has replaced this. In time the peaceful atmosphere of the place will reassert itself.

Chekhov encouraged actors to practise creating atmospheres in their imagination by reading through scenes from plays, getting a sense of the overall atmosphere and then imagining the characters acting and speaking in tune with it. Rather than just doing this once, Chekhov proposes that the exercise is repeated until the inner performance is satisfactory and then suggests altering the atmosphere.

The next phase is to speak and move in harmony with the atmosphere and to begin to radiate the 'inner life' stimulated by the atmosphere back into the space, thereby setting up a kind of feedback loop which amplifies both the atmosphere and the inner response. Once actors develop a basic facility in creating atmospheres they can explore transforming them and breaking them.

The atmosphere and the audience

According to Chekhov the atmosphere of a performance is created by the performers in collaboration with the audience. When a performance starts there is always a specific atmosphere in the theatre which varies from night to night. It depends on the composition of the audience and a number of other things, including what's going on in the world outside of the theatre. If the cast can be open to these differences, then their performance will subtly alter in order that an unspoken rapport can be built between performer and audience. This rapport assists in the establishment of the performance's atmosphere. If there is a different atmosphere in the audience from that onstage, then there is a conflict and Chekhov's assertion – that two objective atmospheres cannot exist in the same space for long – is relevant here. In these circumstances the actors need to be able to transform the atmosphere of the audience. If they fail to do this they run the risk of the performance falling apart or of it being transformed by the atmosphere of the audience. On the other hand, this transformation cannot occur through the performers trying to ignore the atmosphere of the audience or, alternatively, attempting to force change. If we try to force change we are no longer treating the audience as a collaborator but as an enemy to be beaten into submission; this will only create tension in the performers and, possibly, in the audience as well, and this will interfere with the feeling of ease which Chekhov considered to be essential.

Actors have to work together as an ensemble and be:

> united with each other and the audience to create a performance that is an organic whole. How can they do this if they are not enveloped in one Atmosphere?

(Chekhov 1991: 35)

INDIVIDUAL FEELINGS

At the beginning of the section on atmosphere I invited you to imagine a warm, joyful party atmosphere where someone was upset. This exercise required you to focus on two things outside of yourself: an atmosphere and the feelings of a person other than yourself. Both of these will have stirred your feelings to some degree, however subtly, and this was done without asking you to focus on what you were feeling. Unlike Stanislavsky's use of personal memory you were not asked to imagine how you would feel if you were in this character's situation, but to get a sense of how they were feeling. The question which arises from this is: 'How can I imagine being in this person's shoes if I've never been in that position myself?'. A Stanislavskian response might be to ask us to remember a moment where we had those kinds of feelings and to transfer those feelings to this person's situation. Chekhov, however, doesn't see that hunting for the memory of a specific moment is useful.

How do we get feelings for performance?

The problem which Stanislavsky and Chekhov are both attempting to solve is an important one: 'How can the actor access at will the feelings necessary for the performance?'. In everyday life our feelings come in response to the situation we are in, but the stage situation isn't real life and we are responding to a fictitious rather than a real situation (although the stage situation always has a 'real' dimension in the sense that we are there in real space and time with our fellow performers and our audience). The artificial nature of the performance situation means that our feelings don't always come as and when we want them.

So both Stanislavsky and Chekhov are looking for a technique which can be used both in rehearsal and in performance.

In answer to the question as to the most effective technique for tackling this difficulty, Chekhov contrasted the 'emotion memory' approach with his own 'sensation' approach.

Problems with emotion memory

Chekhov identified a number of problems with the emotion memory approach. First, it is a long and involved approach which, while it might produce results in the rehearsal situation, is too complex to be an effective means of awakening our feelings in performance. Chekhov's description of the stages of the emotion memory approach sounds as though it involves digging up a corpse and attempting to revivify it. The actor has to remember and relive a memory, and this involves digging it out of the subconscious and making it 'alive' in the hope that it will 'awaken our artistic feelings' (Powers 1992).

Second, the actor might get stuck in the relived feelings, which will stay around like 'ghosts'. The relived memories, which belong to the actor and not the character, are too tied to the actor's personal life and affect the performance in a way which Chekhov describes as 'unpleasant'. Why does Chekhov describe this as unpleasant? Because he believed that the audience doesn't want to see the performers really suffer – they come to see an artistic event and they expect the feelings to have what he called an 'artistic fragrance'. The audience wants to be engaged in the performance and in the feelings, while at the same time knowing that what's happening on the stage is a fiction. Whether or not we agree with Chekhov's assessment of the audience's expectations, we can see the possibility that reliving our personal memories and experiences might affect our ability to perform as someone different from ourselves.

Third, and connected to the second point, there is the possibility that, by digging up our memories, we might be overwhelmed by the feelings and lose our 'mental balance'. Chekhov prefers not to say much about this either in his books or in his Hollywood lectures of 1955, indicating that it would take us too far into a discussion of psychiatry. Chekhov's concern here is clearly for the well-being of the performer, but there is no sense of the severity of the danger. Even Lee Strasberg, who was the most prominent advocate of the emotion memory approach in the US, recognised this danger and didn't want the actor to work with feelings which were too fresh or raw; so we can see that the dangers of using emotion memory weren't ignored by other practitioners.

Stanislavsky's approach had links to the research of the French psychologist, Théodule Ribot (1839–1916), who identified a link between 'sensation memory' and 'emotion memory'. Ribot believed that all of our past experiences were stored in our bodies, but emotions were harder to recall than the specific sense memories of sound, taste, smell, touch and sight. By remembering specific sense memories, or 'sensations', we might be able to recall emotion memories, but, as Ribot noted, this process is not a speedy one. We have already seen that Michael Chekhov felt that this slowness was a significant disadvantage in performance.

Sensations and qualities

Chekhov claimed that it was part of our nature to forget our experiences and to let them sink into our subconscious, where they are transformed and condensed into what he calls 'sensations' or 'archetypes'. When the performer wants to access emotions it is these archetypes that are accessed, according to Chekhov, rather than any specific memory. Interestingly, this doesn't sound very different from what Stanislavsky writes in *An Actor Prepares*:

> Each of us has seen many accidents. We retain the memories of them, but only outstanding characteristics that impressed us and not their details. Out of these impressions one large, condensed, deeper and broader sensation memory of related experience is formed. It is a kind of synthesis of memory on a large scale. It is purer, more condensed, compact, substantial and sharper than the actual happenings.
>
> *Time is a splendid filter for our remembered feelings – besides it is a great artist. It not only purifies, it also transmutes even painfully realistic memories into poetry.*
>
> (Stanislavsky 1980: 73)

So, Stanislavsky himself appears to accept that we don't work with memories of specific events, but with 'purified' memories. But we're still left with the problem of how to access the feelings we need for our role and Stanislavsky's approach was to start with a specific sense memory in order to get to the store of purified emotion memory.

Chekhov's method is different. He approaches feelings by asking us to do an action with a specific 'quality'. We can take any simple action and do it without difficulty. We can also do the same movement cautiously, or tenderly, or soothingly, or thoughtfully, or fiercely, for example. Chekhov puts this in a very straightforward way: the action is 'what' we're doing and the quality is 'how' we are doing it. Again, we are presented with an approach which we can put to the test immediately.

Experiment with sensations and qualities

In the 1953 version of the book Chekhov explains the process very simply:

> Lift your arm. Lower it. What have you done? You have fulfilled a simple physical *action*. You have made a *gesture*. And you have made it without any difficulty. Why? Because like every action, it is completely within your will. Now make the same gesture, but this time colour it with a certain *quality*. Let this quality be *caution*. You will make your gesture, your movement, *cautiously*. Have you not done it with the same ease? Do it again and again and then see what happens.
>
> (2002: 58)

Try this exercise. What do you notice? Explore moving with different qualities, such as sorrow, calm, grief, irritation, tenderness and ease. Try doing different actions with each of these qualities. What do you notice? Chekhov suggests that, when a quality is added to the action, it ceases being a 'mere physical action', but acquires 'a certain *psychological* nuance' or 'tint'. This is what he calls a 'psychophysical sensation', a sensation which is both physical and psychological. In other words, our feelings are stimulated by adding a quality to our action, and this happens without us having to 'force' our feelings or recall a specific moment when we've experienced a similar feeling before.

Do you find this an easy way to get in touch with your feelings? Don't worry if you notice very little at first – it's a skill which needs to be practised. Once you are beginning to move with your chosen qualities and have become aware of the changes in your psychology, then explore what happens when you allow the qualities to enter into your speech.

Chekhov's elegant and simple technique overcomes the slowness of the emotion memory approach and is suitable for use in performance. It also avoids the dangers of the actor becoming absorbed in, or overwhelmed by, personal feelings. By shifting quickly between different actions and qualities the actor develops a fluidity of feeling on the stage. This is a way of becoming what Artaud called an 'affective athlete', and Chekhov was renowned for his ability to switch quickly from tears to laughter without giving a superficial impression.

THE ACTOR'S BODY

PHYSICAL–PSYCHOLOGICAL EXERCISES

The chapter on the actor's body seems to come at an odd place in *On the Technique of Acting*, perhaps because, for us, the actor's body is often the starting place and because of the importance of the body in Chekhov's own work. As Chekhov points out, however, 'there are no purely physical exercises' (1991: 43) in his technique and the work on imagination, atmosphere and qualities is an all-important aspect of how the actor's body is trained. In *To the Actor*, however, the first chapter is entitled 'The Actor's Body and Psychology', and he states early on that it is important for the actor to attempt to attain a 'complete harmony' between body and psychology (2002: 1). For Chekhov, all performers have to come to terms with their body's 'resistance'. By this he means that, while we might be able to imagine what we want to do and express, we will be unable to do so unless our bodies are appropriately trained. Because the actor is working with atmospheres, feelings and images, a purely physical training, such as gymnastics or acrobatics, is insufficient. The actor requires a training which develops a 'sensitivity of the body to the psychological, creative impulses' (ibid.: 2) and which, at the same time, develops a 'rich, colourful, psychology' – both psychology and body should be under the control of the 'actor'. This interrelationship is at the core of Chekhov's training.

Before we can do anything, we have to have the will to do it. Sometimes everything feels too difficult. We go into the studio and really don't feel up to doing anything – we're almost on automatic pilot, going through the motions. In these moments everything can seem flat and uninteresting, but we know that we really enjoy the work when we get into it. That's why we do it. In this state of mind we can be hard on ourselves, trying to force our enthusiasm, being critical of ourselves or the teacher because we're not feeling alive. What we need is a way of activating our will, a technique which we can remember when we're in the flat space which will get our energy moving in an appropriate way. We also need to be able to ensure that even our smallest movements reverberate energetically throughout our whole body. We also need to be able to do this with a sense of ease. In order to awaken our will and develop our ability to energise the smallest movement, Chekhov suggests that certain gestures can help, and the exercises in this section are about awakening the whole psycho-physical organism that is the actor.

ARCHETYPAL GESTURES

The first exercise described in *To the Actor* involves an action of opening and then closing, of expansion and then contraction. Expanding ourselves to our physical maximum in a star shape without strain, we remain at our fullest (physical) extent, while imagining that we are continuing to expand. This is repeated several times and Chekhov suggests that we say to ourselves 'I am going to awaken the sleeping muscles of my body; I am going to revivify and use them' (2002: 6). This is the aim of the exercise: to awaken our muscles and to make them more sensitive to our needs (and, going the other way, to make us more sensitive to the needs of our muscles – we must beware of overstraining them!). To put it another way, this exercise is one of many that Chekhov uses to awaken us to the energy that is necessary for the actor's work.

Once we've got the sense of expansion, we can then move on to beginning to develop a sense of contraction, perhaps, as Chekhov suggests, by crossing our arms across our chests, going down on to our knees and bowing our heads, while imagining that the space around us is also contracting. Again, once we reach the physical limit of our contraction we continue with the action in our imagination. Because when expanding we were supposed to say to ourselves that we were 'waking', we might imagine that, when we're contracting, we should say to ourselves that we are 'sleeping'; but this isn't so. Both exercises are about awakening our muscles and developing their sensitivity; both are about developing our performer's energy.

These movements of opening and closing are among those Chekhov called 'archetypal gestures'; other ones that he describes are: thrusting, stretching, beating, throwing, lifting, holding, dragging, pushing and tossing. To some extent, these archetypal gestures can be seen as analogous to the eight 'basic effort actions' identified by choreographer and dance educationalist, Rudolf Laban, who was at Dartington during the same period as Chekhov. Laban's eight actions are: pressing, wringing, flicking, dabbing, slashing, gliding, thrusting and floating. Thrusting is the only one to appear in both lists, although, as we shall see, floating has its place in Chekhov's scheme. Laban's effort actions are not descriptions of psychophysical exercises, but they can be added to Chekhov's list and explored in a Chekhovian manner. The point, for Chekhov, is to do these actions clearly and boldly, with a good sense of shape and direction, and to continue the exercise in the imagination after the physical action has completed or reached its limit. Interestingly, in relation to the link I've just made to Laban, Chekhov instructs us to 'avoid dancing movements' (2002: 6).

All of these movements are designed to awaken our energy and develop our sensitivity. After each movement we can return to neutral and have a sense of the action still resonating within.

IDEAL CENTRE

In *On the Technique of Acting,* the chapter on the actor's body opens with the exercise on discovering the imaginary centre in the chest, while in *To the Actor* this comes after the exercises listed above.

Chekhov wants us to imagine that there is a centre in the middle of our chest which is the 'source' of our 'energy and power' (2002: 7), and that we are to imagine as we move that all of our impulses flow from this centre and that our movements are filled with energy flowing from it through to the tips of our fingers and toes. This is an exercise to get us to release our joints and unblock the flow of energy, which is essential to developing a feeling of ease in performance. By imagining that our legs and arms receive impulses from this centre, Chekhov suggests that we can unlock our hips and shoulders. Imagining that our arms and our legs begin in this centre (which brings quite a grotesque image to mind!), we can explore doing everyday activities with a sense that an impulse of energy from this centre precedes the action. In fact, Chekhov suggests that we imagine the centre itself going out in front of the body and then follow it. Once the action is completed don't let the energy drop but imagine it continuing to radiate out. This is related to the sense in the previous exercise where, when we returned to neutral, we had a sense of the action still resonating inside – only this time the emphasis is on going out rather than listening in. Another way of thinking about it is to return to the exercises in expansion and contraction at the beginning of this section. When we are expanding, our imagination continues the action outwards, while, when we are contracting, we continue the action inwardly.

At this point the exercise is about developing a sense of power and ease in movement. Later Chekhov discusses the relationship between the different centres and characterisation. The centre in the middle of the chest is, for Chekhov, an 'ideal' centre that is part of his ideal actor's body. Eugenio Barba, who has conducted much research into the ways in which actors learn to develop an effective stage presence, notes that every performance tradition locates the key centre in a different part of the body and that it makes little sense to argue about which is the 'true' centre. What is important, according to Barba, is that this centre is located precisely and deliberately and is:

> mentally and therefore physically effective, different from the points at which, in daily action, movements seem to begin (joints, muscles).
>
> (1995: 75)

The point here is that we are to imagine that the energetic source of our actions is different from how we normally conceive it in daily life. Even though the actor may be attempting to represent daily life, this is done on the basis of an artistic technique. Chekhov wants us to keep this in mind.

MOULDING, FLOWING, FLYING AND RADIATING

The next group of exercises which Chekhov proposes as a means of developing the actor's technique are based on the four elements: earth ('moulding'), water ('flowing'), air ('flying') and fire ('radiating'). In *To the Actor* the exercise in flowing is called 'floating', but 'flowing' is the more accurate term and there is another exercise in floating which has a different feeling altogether. All of these exercises are, once again, psychophysical and involve the engagement of the imagination. At first these movements can be explored without paying attention to the 'ideal' centre – Chekhov was concerned not to overload students by asking them to do too much at once. When we have become more familiar with the exercises, Chekhov recommends that we keep a sense of the movements beginning in the chest centre.

Moulding

This exercise involves making broad movements, while imagining that we're moulding the space like a sculptor working clay. The idea is to get a sense that each movement leaves a clear and definite impression in the air. This involves imagining that the air resists our movement, but we must avoid unnecessary muscular tension. Everything must be done with a feeling of ease. Each movement needs to have a clear beginning, middle and end.

Once again Chekhov wants us to repeat the movements to get a stronger sense of the form of each and of the impression we're leaving behind. We need to set ourselves the task of making each gesture clearer and more precise, or of acknowledging the clarity it had in the first place and then being able to maintain it through numerous repetitions. Then we are to explore moulding the same shapes using different parts of our bodies.

Once we are comfortable with large movements, Chekhov encourages us to work with everyday actions and then to focus down on to the fingers and imagine even the smallest movement as leaving an impression in the space.

Through this exercise in moulding, Chekhov hoped that students would develop a sense of the importance of form for the actor and learn to be dissatisfied with 'vague and shapeless' work in themselves and in others. One benefit of working in this way is that we can learn to direct the audience's attention to where we want it, filling even the smallest movement with the same energy, or power, as a large one and ensuring that the signal we are sending, however subtle, has a clarity of form.

Flowing

In flowing, all our movements, while they still have a definite shape, merge into each other – there is no beginning, middle and end, just a continuous flow. However, because these movements are inspired by the element of water, Chekhov wants us to imagine the movement 'growing and subsiding' like the waves on the sea. At the same time we are not to be submerged in the water, but to imagine that we are supported on the surface. As with moulding, we start with large movements and then explore making the movements with different parts of the body; then we experiment with doing everyday activities with the same quality. In *To the Actor*, there is the suggestion that we should pause every few minutes while exploring flowing, in order to reflect on what we've done and to sense the effect that the movements have had on us. This is, once again, a means of getting us to pay attention to the internal resonance of an action. Chekhov claims that, if we do this after making flowing movements, we will get a sensation of 'calm, poise and psychological warmth' (2002: 10).

Flying

In this exercise we have to imagine that each of our movements flies away from us and continues indefinitely, while at the same time the body 'has a tendency to lift itself from the ground' (Chekhov 1991: 46). Flying movements are always expanding outwards and upwards. In order to get a sense of this there must be an outer pause at the end of each movement as we imagine it continuing out into space. Imagine throwing a stone to the moon. That would be an amazing throw and not physically possible, but in the imagination anything is possible. Take an imaginary stone and throw it, aiming for the moon. When your arm reaches its full extension and at the moment you imagine releasing the stone, pause, holding the position and imagining the stone continuing on to the moon. You'll need to pay close attention to what you're doing – it's quite common, when trying this exercise for the first time, to pause in a position a few moments after the stone was released. It's important that you give your imaginary stone a clear direction!

Once again, this can be done with large whole-body movements, with different parts of the body, and in the process of doing everyday actions. Chekhov suggests that we will get a sense of lightness and ease from this exercise.

Radiating

This exercise is related to the one used when exploring the ideal centre. Chekhov gives a description of what he means:

> Lift your arm, lower it, stretch it forward, sideways; walk around the room, lie down, sit down, get up, etc.; but continuously and in advance send the rays from your body into the space around you, in the direction of the movement you make and after the movement is made.
>
> (2002: 11)

But it still might be unclear what Chekhov means by 'rays'. Our bodies radiate energy. In a simple, everyday sense we can, for example, verify that they radiate heat. In our imaginations it isn't difficult to grasp the idea that we also radiate different qualities of light. Nor is it unusual to say that someone is looking 'radiant', or that they are in a 'sombre mood'. Chekhov, however, is going a little further than this and drawing attention to the idea that all living things possess an energy body, or a radiant energy field which is interwoven with the physical body. While Chekhov was at the First Studio in Moscow, Sulerzhitsky conducted experiments with 'prana', which he understood to be the Sanskrit word used in yoga to describe this energy field. Students would attempt to channel the prana through their fingertips or their eyes and make contact with their partners, who had their backs to them, through the energy. The aim of these experiments was to develop the actor's ability to radiate and direct this energy, both to other actors onstage and to the audience.

Chekhov isn't suggesting here that the energy only be radiated through the fingertips and the eyes but, first, through the whole body, and then through the different parts. Again this can be explored with the chest centre as the source of the radiation.

Aware that this work with radiation might prove difficult, Chekhov offers the following words of advice:

> You must not be disturbed by doubts as to whether you are actually radiating or whether you are only imagining that you are. If you sincerely and convincingly imagine that you are sending out rays, the imagination will gradually and faithfully lead you to the real and actual process of radiating.
>
> (2002: 12)

In a sense this is true of all of Chekhov's exercises: we can easily begin to doubt whether or not they're working, but it is the doubt itself that gets in the way. We need to put our doubts aside while we engage with the exercise, and reflect on whether we achieved what we set out to do afterwards.

If we think of radiating as the giving out of energy, then we can see that receiving is its opposite. We need to be able to receive whatever is significant from our fellow performers and our environment, and this includes words, actions, atmospheres, events, etc. But, once again, Chekhov requires that we don't take this idea of receiving for granted. He considers that it is not just a matter of 'looking and listening', but an active drawing in of what's around us. We can relate this back to the ideas of expansion and contraction. When we were exploring expansion, we were imagining our energy extending out beyond the physical limit of our action; but when we were contracting, we were imagining the energy being drawn inwards. This opposition of radiating and receiving, expanding and contracting provides a dynamic pulse at the heart of an actor's performance.

There are no moments onstage when we are not either giving or receiving according to Chekhov's model. We are always connected, however subtly, to our fellow performers, the set and the audience.

THE FOUR BROTHERS

A group of exercises known as the 'four brothers' are important because they focus on qualities which relate to all other work in the Chekhov technique. They are 'the feeling of ease', 'the feeling of the whole', 'the feeling of form' and 'the feeling of beauty'. Interestingly the four are not grouped together in *On the Technique of Acting* where only ease, form and beauty are discussed in the chapter on the actor's body. All four are present in *To the Actor*, where 'the feeling of the whole' is referred to as 'the quality of entirety'.

The feeling of ease

The feeling of ease involves performing any action with a sense of lightness and ease, no matter how 'heavy' the theme. This enables us to keep a distinction between the character and the actor: the character may be suffering great torment, but the actor is to represent all of this

Figure 2.2
Chekhov's
students at
work in the
garden at
Dartington

with a light touch. This quality of ease replaces Stanislavsky's exercises in relaxation and Chekhov considered it to be a crucial aspect of art and connected to humour. Chekhov states that the quality of ease can best be achieved through the exercises of flying and radiating. Return to those exercises and note whether or not you're doing them with this quality of ease and lightness.

The feeling of form

Again Chekhov distinguishes between the theme and the quality of the actor's representation of the theme. For example, we might be dealing with a chaotic situation or with a character who is a 'bewildered, chaotic type of man with no sense of form' (Chekhov 2002: 14), but the actor must be able to give shape to this chaos. The character may be a mess, but this shouldn't be confused with a messy performance. Chekhov refers us back to the exercise in moulding and to the idea that every movement must have a clear beginning and ending. By focusing on the forms we create, Chekhov thought that the actor would develop a good awareness of how we move the whole of our body, including our finger-tips and toes, and that this would help not only in the development of a character, but also in the development of the actor as a creative artist. While this awareness of form gives us a sense of distance that enables us to observe our movements as artistic forms, Chekhov warns against becoming too distant. We mustn't lose a sense of inner connection to the movements.

While working with a sense of form, Chekhov suggests that we should be clear about the intended action and its quality before we do it, for only then will we know whether or not we've achieved what we set out to do and be able to make informed adjustments.

The feeling of beauty

This is an inner sense which involves a feeling of deep satisfaction in the work and is to be distinguished from 'showing off'. Chekhov gives the example of someone profoundly engaged in a physical task and flowing effortlessly. One exercise Chekhov suggests to approach this sense of beauty is quite a subtle one: he invites us to make simple movements and to pay attention to the sense of pleasure we feel while moving. We're not to try and show it, or make the movements beautiful or pleasurable for someone else, just to notice the pleasure that arises, however subtle it may be. This is another way of keeping alive our sense of being creative artists. When we are enacting scenes of pain or violence, Chekhov believed that we needed the sense of beauty to help us stay aware that what we are creating is a piece of art, not real life.

The feeling of the whole/entirety

The feeling of the whole, or of entirety, is closely related to the feeling of form and can perhaps be best understood as looking at forms in the wider context. If we take all of the actions we, or our character, makes throughout the whole of the performance, and try to see how they connect with each other to give a sense of the whole, or entire, performance, then we are working with the feeling of the whole. We can make this even more complex by adding the actions of all of the other characters in the performance and the contexts in which these actions are made, and this will help us not only have a grasp of our own work and how it fits into the whole, but also the work of others. As we begin to develop this more complex viewpoint, we begin to approach the kind of perspective that Chekhov felt a creative director should have.

One exercise Chekhov offers to help us understand and develop the feeling of the whole is to reflect on the events of our day and to select those sections that appear to have a sense of completion – their own beginning, middle and end. We need to go over them in our mind's eye until we have a good clear sense of the form of each one, and then try to gain a sense of how they all fit together and an impression of the shape of the whole day. Once we've explored that, we can go on to consider the whole of our life in this fashion, imagining the shape it might have in the future. Then we can apply this exercise to a folk tale, novel or play.

THE ACTOR'S THREEFOLD BODY

Chekhov uses a threefold model of the human body drawn from the work of Rudolf Steiner. The body is divided into three interlinked parts, which are also related to specific psychological/emotional qualities. The first is the head, which is connected to thinking and ideas;

the second includes the chest and the arms and is connected to feelings and, through our breathing and heartbeat, to our sense of rhythm. The third part comprises our legs and feet and is connected to our will; the job of our legs is to move us through space according to our feelings and ideas.

The head

Like Edward Gordon Craig, Chekhov was very critical of the way western actors used their faces. Craig described the use of the face by actors since the Renaissance as 'spasmodic and ridiculous' (1980: 13) and suggested that the only artistic solution was to use masks. Chekhov, on the other hand, thought that the actor had to stop forcing expression and allow the face to radiate the actor's 'affections and moods' (1991: 52). Both men were, however, concerned that the actor's use of the face in their time was inartistic and that this had to be changed. Once again, we're engaging with the idea of the actor's habits and the need to examine them. If, as a result of our experience, we should come to different conclusions from Chekhov and Craig, we would still have to have become aware of how the face is used, by ourselves and by others, and come to an evaluation of its effectiveness. By raising our awareness of this issue we already move beyond the position of the actors that Chekhov is challenging.

The chest

The idea that our chest is linked to our feelings is quite a common one. What's perhaps less common is Chekhov's sense of the relationship between rhythm and feeling. Concerned that we weren't overwhelmed by our emotions and that emotion was always expressed artistically, Chekhov sees this linking of rhythm to feeling as a means of artistic control. Not only can we move with a specific quality (e.g. sadness), but we can also explore the rhythm of that quality to give us a richer awareness of its composition. Ultimately, it doesn't matter where we start from, because the different aspects of the quality appear together. If we move our arms with a quality of sadness, there is already a particular rhythm involved, but by exploring rhythm we can have a greater sense of the quality.

The legs and feet

Our will involves our capacity to make decisions for action and to carry them out. The way in which we carry out these actions tells us something about the quality of our will. We might be strong-willed, or weak-willed which are common ways of thinking about the will. Or we might have a soft, gentle will; a hard, forceful will; or a curious, anxious, joyful or sleepy will. Any of the qualities we looked at earlier can be applied to the will. A will can be very strong at the beginning of an action but peter out before the end. In the middle of an argument, for example, someone decides to leave and strides forcefully towards the door, but their will softens just before they reach it. The initial choice to leave is clear, but as the door is approached there is perhaps a desire to stay that comes into conflict with the choice to leave, or perhaps a fear of the consequences of leaving at this point weakens the will. Whatever desire and quality, the will needs to be seen, according to Chekhov, in the legs and in the feet. He comments on how often actors don't seem to know what to do with their feet and how they pace around the stage without a sense of purpose. Paying attention to the character's will and how it's manifested in the legs and feet helps us to be clear about how and why we're travelling in the space.

Of course the will is not only to be found in the legs and the feet, no more than the feelings are only to be found in the chest and arms, but this way of looking at things enables us to consider how we're using our limbs as part of our overall performance.

We've gone quite deeply into Chekhov's thoughts on acting and the means he proposed to achieve his goal. Of course there is far too much to take in everything in one go, and the exercises themselves need practice, but we're now ready to move on to what is, perhaps, Chekhov's single most original contribution to twentieth-century actor training: the 'psychological gesture'.

THE PSYCHOLOGICAL GESTURE

The work in all of the previous exercises provides a basis for developing the psychological gesture (PG) and, in fact, the archetypal gestures explored earlier are already a form of it.

THE PSYCHOLOGICAL GESTURE AND WILLPOWER

A PG needs to be strong, clear and simple. Initially, it is an exercise to awaken us to our willpower and to prepare us for creative work. It is no good if we are half-hearted; we need to be fully engaged with our action. Without the willpower to engage in the training we will fall by the wayside. You will have noticed that I haven't mentioned anything about the kind of movement (that is, its shape, or form), nor anything about its quality.

Let's go back to the expanding and contracting movements discussed earlier. Remember that, whether we were expanding or contracting, the aim of these different kinds of movement was to wake us up. It is possible, however, that each of these movements awakened a different desire: to reach to the stars or to hide in a shell, for example. Try the exercise again and see if any desire comes to you: what 'want' is awakened by this action? The same gesture can generate different wants in different people and in the same people at different times; there is no 'right' or 'wrong' in terms of the meaning that each maker of the gesture creates.

Once we have the desire associated with a particular movement, we can explore doing it with different qualities to awaken our feelings. Of course, each movement will have had a specific quality when we first did it – it can't not – but now we have the opportunity to look at it more closely and to make adjustments.

Any kind of movement can be material for a PG, as long as it strong, clear, simple and engages our will, desire and feelings. But it is more than that. The PG is a means of expressing the entire character in condensed form through an intuitive grasp of the character's main desire. When we read a play, or a story, we develop an intuitive sense of the character which might be difficult to analyse. Chekhov wants us to work with this intuition and to ask 'what the main desire of the character might be' (2002: 67). What's this character's main aim? This idea of a 'main desire' is what Stanislavsky calls the 'objective', but Chekhov's approach is more intuitive than his teacher's. It's also important to note that two characters could have identical objectives but very different PGs. The objective, simply phrased as 'I want to win the fight', tells us nothing about how this want appears in any specific character. The PG is always an expression of an a character's objective as part of their individual psychology.

Choosing a key moment

Chekhov suggests that we focus on a key moment in our imagination and watch the character to try to get a sense of what their objective is. Perhaps we only have a vague sense of what it might be, but we make a tentative movement with our hand and see if we get a sense of what the character wants, the desire. Again, there's no right or wrong. We need to check back with the character in our imagination and see whether the gesture works for us and keep building, and adjusting if necessary, until the whole body is involved in the gesture. You might be able to do that from the beginning or you might need to build it up step by step, it doesn't matter – we have to find our own way through the exercises according to our own needs. The aim, however, is the same: to get our whole self engaged in the psychological gesture. Once you've found a PG you still might feel that it isn't quite right for your character, so try another one. Chekhov's answer to the question, 'How do I know if I've got the right PG?', is 'It is right if it satisfies you as an artist' (2002: 69). This use of the PG is to get a sense of the essence of the character you're working with and to provide a quick and effective way of getting in touch with the character before going onstage.

THE PSYCHOLOGICAL GESTURE AND LANGUAGE

While we are invited to find a PG for our entire role, there is also the possibility of finding PGs for smaller sections of the role. One way of approaching this is through language. Drawing on the work of Steiner, Chekhov notes that we often use gestural language when talking of psychological processes. For example, we 'grow pensive', 'draw conclusions' or 'grasp ideas'. Chekhov considers that these phrases suggest that a 'tendency to produce such a gesture' (1991: 59) exists at these moments and can stimulate us to make the physical gesture if necessary. Let's take the idea of 'falling in love' as an example. If we focus for a moment on this phrase, what kind of gesture comes to us? Explore it for a while, making the action as clear as possible. Once you feel you've got the gesture that works for your sense of falling in love, repeat it as an internal action – in other words, just do it in your imagination. Now, keeping that sense of inner action, speak the line: 'I want to go home!' Try to speak the words in tune with the inner gesture.

Try 'falling asleep' and 'falling into despair' and repeat the whole exercise for each, including the words. Can you sense if the words take on a different meaning as you speak them with a different PG?

I could have just asked you to say the line 'as if' you were falling in love, into despair, or asleep. That would have encouraged you to draw on something you already know in an ordinary, everyday sense. Chekhov thought that this would just lead to us playing our own clichés and not help us to discover our own creative individuality. What do you think would have been the difference if I'd asked you to speak the line with the quality of 'falling in love'?

We can find the smaller PGs for lines in the text, for single words, or for the gaps between words – wherever we get a sense that our character has a different want. But all these little PGs are still informed by the overall PG, the one that sums up the major aim of the character. As Chekhov says:

> Each character on the stage has one main desire, and one characteristic manner of fulfilling this desire. Whatever variations the character may show during the play in pursuing this desire, he nevertheless always remains the same character.

(1991: 90)

PUTTING IT ALL TOGETHER

Once we start exploring these mini PGs we could go on for ever, finding smaller and smaller sections to investigate. But that would be to miss the point. The PG is there to help us develop our understanding of the internal dynamics of our character and, once we have used the minor ones to help with our process of discovery, they can disappear into the flow of our performance. We don't even have to make conscious use of the overarching PG unless we need to, perhaps before our entrances, or because we're playing more than one character and want to be sure that we're keeping them distinct.

It doesn't really matter when in the process we arrive at the PG. It's not a case of saying that by week three of rehearsals all performers should have their overall PG in place, even if we might want to work that way as an experiment. In fact, even if we don't ever get a clear PG, it doesn't mean that we're failures. I once heard Hurd Hatfield, an ex-student of Chekhov, who has had a very successful stage and screen career, say that, although he thought he understood the idea of the PG, he never used it. On the other hand, actors such as Sir Anthony Hopkins, Clint Eastwood and Jack Nicholson have found it very useful. The only way to know if it works for you is to explore it.

One important question is whether the PG is ever visible to the audience. Chekhov's writings often suggest that it should be invisible, although this appears to some extent to depend on the style of performance undertaken, and Chekhov uses the term to refer to 'visible (actual) gestures as well as to invisible (potential) gestures' (1991: 60).

INCORPORATION AND CHARACTERISATION

At some point we must begin to take on the character. One of the key things in Chekhov's thinking about acting is that there are no 'straight' parts, no roles in which we are just ourselves. Why is this? Because Chekhov believed that no two people are alike and that it is the differences between us that allow us to think of characters. If I'm always 'me' onstage, what happens to the character? Yes, my Hamlet will be different from yours, but my Hamlet needs to be different from me in everyday life and also different from my Macbeth. We are always looking for what's different between the character we are going to play and ourselves. Chekhov claims that, whether we know it or not, we have a 'deeply rooted . . . desire for transformation'. We want to transform ourselves into the character. Without this desire we can't really like acting!

THE IMAGINARY BODY

Chekhov has proposed many different exercises to help us embody the character. One of these is to imagine the character's body outside of yourself, in as much detail as possible, and then to step into it. You can wear the different body as if it were a different costume.

For some people, stepping into an imaginary body might be quite simple, but for others it can be extremely difficult, even after lots of preparatory work. Chekhov acknowledges that moving into the imaginary body too soon can be quite shocking and suggests taking on the body in parts, perhaps starting with the hands, or the feet, or the nose. Eventually we take on the whole of the character's body, which is different from ours in significant ways. There are limits to how much difference we can manage, but it's fun to explore those limits to find out where they are.

One thing to explore is stepping in and out of the imaginary body until you can do it with ease – something which is especially useful if you're playing more than one character in a performance and need to make quick shifts. From Chekhov's perspective, we need to take care that our representation of the character isn't superficial, so we have to continue to develop our sense of the character's feelings and will. One way of doing this is just to practise with the imaginary body, becoming more and more at home in it and allowing thoughts and feelings to emerge. This should all be done with a sense of ease.

HOW DOES OUR IMAGINATION GET ITS INFORMATION?

One question is: How does our imagination get the information it needs to construct the imaginary body and its details in the first place? One way of thinking about this is to remember the discussion on dreams and how our subconscious creates new images out of the experiences we've had during the day. These experiences include stories we've read, films we've watched and artwork we've encountered, as well as our experience of crossing a road or seeing someone we love or who frightens us. All of this material is there for our subconscious artist to draw on.

As we consciously conduct the exercises and the experiments that Chekhov suggests, we continue to supply material which can be drawn on later. This doesn't just involve conscious work in class, but also outside. We need to become aware of atmospheres around us, as we've already noted, but we also need to pay attention to the things that people do, their specific gestures and tones of voice, their habitual actions and their idiosyncrasies. Chekhov insists that we do this with an open mind – with a sense of wonder and curiosity rather than criticism. According to Chekhov's theory, all of this information is then stored in our subconscious as material which can be used in our work. The idea isn't that we observe someone doing a particular action in some detail and that we then play this person as a character at some future date. Rather, that this material will emerge as part of a character when it's appropriate.

IMAGINARY CENTRES

We met what Chekhov called the 'ideal centre' earlier: a centre in the chest from which we imagined our movement flowed. This was Chekhov's ideal actor's body. But each character will have a different centre and Chekhov considered that, by discovering these centres, we could further develop our characterisation.

You might already have some experience of working with centres. For example, there is an exercise sometimes used in physical theatre training, where the actor walks across the space placing the centre in different parts of the body: nose, mouth, chest, stomach, groin, knees and feet. If you've tried this exercise you'll remember that you had to get a sense of each of these centres leading you across the space. (If you haven't tried it, there's something else to explore!)

Chekhov's exploration of centres was far more detailed than this. An imaginary centre can be visualised anywhere in the body. Once we've placed the imaginary centre, we can imagine that all of the character's energy radiates from this point. You can experiment with this by imagining that your centre is in your left eye, or your stomach, or the back of your neck, and by imagining that all of your energy centres on that point. Spend a few moments doing this before moving on.

All that we did in the exercise above was imagine that the centre of energy in the body was in different places. Chekhov suggested that we explore this in even more detail by giving different qualities to the centre. How is it different, for example, if you imagine a hard, tight, dark centre in your left eye? Or a large, soft centre in your stomach? What if the centre is sharp and thin, like a needle at the end of your nose?

Like the psychological gesture, the imaginary centre is used for the character as a whole, but can also be used for sections of the role. While the overall centre is the home, or default setting, for the character, the energy might be centred at different places at different moments in the performance.

Chekhov sets an exercise of creating five different characters in half an hour using the imaginary body and centre method. In addition, we have to find their characteristic voice and actions. Give it a try. You can jump into the imaginary body as a whole or try it on in small bits, whatever best suits your way of working.

I mentioned earlier that some people have said that they don't find the psychological gesture approach useful. In some ways, the work with the imaginary body and centres seems more straightforward. Which feels easiest for you? Whichever it is, perhaps you're trying too hard with the other one. Next time, try approaching the more difficult approach with a feeling of ease and see if it makes any difference.

CHARACTERISATION

What Chekhov means by characterisation is the addition of small, idiosyncratic features of the character. This is distinct from the sense of the character as a whole that we get through the initial work on the imaginary body. It might be, for example, a way of tilting the head when trying to remember something, or a way of smiling in particular situations. These are small 'finishing touches', which may appear at different points in the process. They might, for example, come from the work on the imaginary centre.

CONCLUSION

Throughout most of *On the Technique of Acting* and *To the Actor*, Chekhov focuses on the work of the individual actor. The sense of the group is always in the background, but the main objective of the book is to help the individual to gain access to their own creative individuality. In *To The Actor* Chekhov includes some ensemble exercises quite early on (Chapter 3), but in *On the Technique of Acting* these have been moved towards the end, where Chekhov begins to describe the process of putting on a play and the stages of the creative process. I'll save discussion of some of the material there for the next two chapters.

3

CHEKHOV AS DIRECTOR

CHOOSING THE FOCUS

Michael Chekhov's career moves through different phases and one way of looking at these is in terms of the roles of actor, director and teacher. As his career progressed each of these became more important in turn, although the others didn't disappear altogether. By the time Chekhov moved to Dartington, it was the teacher and director roles which were dominant, and the same was true while the Chekhov Studio was at Ridgefield. Chekhov did consider playing King Lear in the Studio production, but eventually decided against it. By the time he moved to Hollywood, the stage actor had pretty much disappeared, although he enjoyed his film acting. Chekhov the director had also faded and Chekhov the teacher was very much to the fore. Of course, from Chekhov's perspective, these can all be seen as aspects of Chekhov the artist and as an expression of his creative individuality; we might also add to these roles Chekhov as author, designer and graphic artist.

Which of these roles is most useful for us in understanding Chekhov's practice? Should we be focusing on Chekhov the actor and his great stage roles? Should we be looking in detail at Chekhov's performance as Khlestakov in Stanislavsky's production of *The Government Inspector*? Or at his performance as Erik XIV in Vakhtangov's production? If we take this route aren't we then only focusing on an individual actor's technique, rather than on the production as a whole?

How do we separate out the work of the director, Stanislavsky or Vakhtangov, from the work of the actor? Then again, what about his performance as Hamlet, in which he was both actor and director? This combination of roles was something which he was later to say was too difficult to do and was the main reason he gave for not taking a minor part in *The Possessed*. If we focus on Chekhov the actor, then, we lose the sense of the production as a whole, and that's of vital importance if we're to understand how Chekhov's work pans out in production, rather than just how an individual actor can develop a role within a production.

Would it be better, then, for us to focus on the work of Chekhov the director and analyse one of the productions he did after he left Russia? One of the problems with this approach is that Chekhov was constantly working with actors who weren't trained in his technique and in rehearsal periods that were too short for training them. This inevitably meant that the best Chekhov could do would be to get the outer form of the performance he was after. The work he did with the Habima was, perhaps, an exception to this, as the actors had previously worked with Vakhtangov and had been working together for a number of years by the time Chekhov directed them in *Twelfth Night*. We have already noted that, when Habima brought Chekhov's production of *Twelfth Night* to London in 1932, John Gielgud was greatly impressed. So we know that, when he was working with a group of experienced actors, especially those used to working in a manner for which he had great respect, Chekhov was an accomplished director. But we don't have, in the Habima production, the combination of Chekhov as teacher and director; that is, we don't have the evidence that the two things go together. To focus on this production of *Twelfth Night* wouldn't help us to understand the relationship between Chekhov's teaching and the processes of putting on a play.

The work that comes out of the Chekhov Studio Theatre in Ridgefield does show us Chekhov the director working with a group of performers that he's trained, yet the group doesn't stay together long enough for the ensemble to be fairly compared with any of the other major ensembles of the twentieth century. That is, despite the critical recognition of the Chekhov Theatre Studio's productions of *Twelfth Night* and *King Lear*, the company didn't really mature as a unit, and Chekhov is viewed as a director of classic plays rather than of new work. This is also something worth noting, because, despite Chekhov's vision of a new theatre with new works, his success as a director after leaving Russia is based primarily on his work with the classics. *The Possessed* is an important production because it was the first public production of the Studio, but the company were very inexperienced and not really skilled enough to model Chekhov's method at its full potential; although, as we shall see below, the reviews were mixed and some-times contradictory. Chekhov's adaptation of *The Pickwick Papers* didn't reach the stage, although rehearsals and workshops took place and Chekhov left behind both a draft script and some detailed director's notes. There are also notes, published in Leonard (1984), which refer to Chekhov's 1946 Hollywood production of *The Government Inspector*, but this isn't a document of a single production – more a collection of ideas and reflections on how to approach the direction of the play.

A third approach would be to look at Chekhov the teacher in rela-tion to scenes and short plays worked on in the classes. These are pieces not intended for public presentation. The difficulty here is that, if we focus too much on the teaching, even though it contains the essential ingredients of what Chekhov wanted in public performance, we don't get any sense of how this work is received by an audience. If we stick with Studio work, we never get a sense of how our work is received by the wider public and what information this reception gives us about our work. Do people understand what we're doing? Does their criticism demonstrate an understanding of our work which stimulates us to develop it further? Have they missed the point alto-gether? Are we playing in the right venues? Are we attracting an appropriate audience?

In the circumstances, the best approach is to examine Chekhov's productions with his students. In these productions Chekhov the teacher of acting comes together with Chekhov the director and we can begin to get a sense of how his theories panned out in public performances and how they were received by the critics. The first of these productions after the school moved to Ridgefield was *The Possessed*, which is generally regarded as an artistic and commercial failure.

THE POSSESSED (1939)

The Chekhov Theatre Studio production of *The Possessed,* which was scripted by George Shdanoff (1905–88) and directed by Chekhov, opened on Broadway at the Lyceum Theatre on 24 October 1939. Initially, Chekhov had planned to work on *The Possessed* and *Pickwick* simultaneously, but early in 1939 he decided that they must concentrate on *The Possessed* in order to get a production on Broadway as soon as possible. What was the urgency? Chekhov was disappointed with the number and quality of new applicants for the Studio at Ridgefield and wanted to establish his work on Broadway, so that the company's reputation would attract new students. He felt that it wouldn't be possible to run the school on its own without some income from a good run on Broadway. This meant working on the production even if it led to the work of the school being neglected.

THE TEXT

Chekhov and Shdanoff started work on *The Possessed* while the school was still based at Dartington, but the move to Ridgefield interrupted the process. The play, which is based on the writings of Fyodor Dostoevsky and, primarily, the 700-page novel of the same name (but which is also translated as *Demons*), is in fifteen relatively short scenes. Shdanoff had written stage adaptations of other novels by Dostoevsky, including *Crime and Punishment* for **Gaston Baty**, which ran for two years in Paris. He had also been credited as co-director, with Alexander Trivas, of a German film, *No Man's Land* (1931), which is regarded as one of the best anti-war films ever made.

Chekhov and Shdanoff's aim wasn't to make a strict adaptation of Dostoevsky's text, but to use Dostoevsky's ideas as a stimulus for 'writing a play which would reflect our modern problems' (Byckling 1995: 33). This was why, when it was only possible to work on one of his planned productions, Chekhov chose *The Possessed* over *Pickwick*: the material was better suited to dealing with the violence of the contemporary world. Millions had died in Russia and, with the aggressive rise of Hitler and the Nazis in Germany, Chekhov realised that the coming war was going to cause the deaths of millions more.

Gaston Baty (1885–1952): director credited with introducing expressionist staging to the French theatre.

DEVISING PROCESS

Although there was a text of the play published to accompany the production, it would be a mistake to regard this as a script that pre-existed the rehearsal process. The script itself evolves out of the interaction between writer, director and actors and, as such, *The Possessed* is a form of devised theatre. Shdanoff would write some text as a basis for improvisations and then rewrite in response to what happened in the studio. This was quite an unusual process in the 1930s, but one which, although still relatively uncommon, has become a well-established approach. It is Shdanoff's name which appears as author on the published text, something which seems to downplay the role of the actors in the creation of the text, but this has also become established as part and parcel of this kind of approach to devised work. A good contemporary example would be the work of British writer/director, Mike Leigh (b. 1943), whose plays and films are based on the improvisations of actors that he writes down and then publishes under his own name.

This was very much Chekhov and Shdanoff's project, despite the fact that the actors were involved in the development of the script through their engagement in improvisations. The actors were discouraged from reading Dostoevsky's novel (Byckling 1995: 34) and didn't have the kind of experience of political violence that was all too familiar to Chekhov. They had to bring their imaginations to the actions suggested by the text and the director and not try to make a performance based on their personal experiences of mass violence, which they didn't have, or their experience of Dostoevsky. It's difficult to understand why Chekhov discouraged the actors from reading Dostoevsky, because it would seem to be an appropriate manner of feeding their subconscious with information that would be useful in the rehearsal process. Reading not only *The Possessed* but other novels of Dostoevsky would have enabled them to get a sense of the atmosphere and style of the novelist's world, including his use of humour and the grotesque. Perhaps Chekhov felt that there was insufficient time with everything else the actors had to absorb. While Chekhov was clear that he wasn't creating a strict adaptation of *The Possessed*, the main storyline and themes of Dostoevsky's novel are clearly in the published playtext. This suggests that, had the actors read Dostoevsky, it wouldn't have affected their understanding. On the other hand, if the only indication of character the actors were receiving was through the rehearsal process, they couldn't come with a preconception of what the character should be like. In one sense this helps the actor be free from the text, while in another it leaves the actor at the mercy of the director. A risk here is that the actors might not feel any ownership of the material and, if they are inexperienced, they might be trying too hard to please the director, rather than engaging in a dialogue with the director's vision and their own creative individuality.

Why draw attention to this? Because Chekhov, in his books on acting, suggests that everyone should read the text and get to know it thoroughly, allowing their imagination to develop. If the individual actor's vision of the play is different from the director's, then the individual must, according to Chekhov, work to fulfil the director's objectives. But the actors must also be able to find the gaps in the direction to use their own creativity. While Chekhov respected the role of the director, he was very much opposed to the director being a dictator, however benevolent. On the other hand, his desire to work with a writer demonstrated a lack of faith in the actors' ability to develop and organise their own performance material. Perhaps this lack of faith grew out of frustrations with student work at Dartington, where students were required to devise their performances on the basis of short stories and folk tales. Certainly we know that Chekhov was unhappy with the work achieved at Dartington, feeling that his teaching was too complicated, but also that the students didn't work hard enough to master the technique and would forget what they'd learned in class once they got on the stage. But we must also remember the situation: that Chekhov had a group of student actors and he was going to put them on the Broadway stage. It would have been extremely risky to rely on the devising skills of an inexperienced group. Devising on the basis of folk tales in the school with an invited audience is one thing; putting an untried group of actors onstage with a weak text in a mainstream theatre is something else altogether.

THE CRITICS AND THE TEXT

Chekhov was concerned that there was appropriate material for the actors to work with, and he had failed to attract audiences with his production based on a folk tale, *The Castle Awakens*, in Paris. So, there was little chance that this kind of material would be successful in New

York, which was much more conservative at this time. But, at the same time, he wanted to work with new material rather than the classics. The irony is that the text of *The Possessed* found very little favour with the New York critics. John Mason Brown of *The New York Post,* for example, felt that the text was so bad that the company couldn't have found a worse one if they'd tried (25 October 1939).

Burns Mantle, in the *Daily News* (25 October 1939), admitted to not really understanding the play – that it seemed to be all about the search for a leader who decided not to lead. But the problem Chekhov was engaging with wasn't whether or not people need leaders, but what kind of leaders were necessary. *The Possessed* puts forward the quite simple idea that those leaders who are 'possessed' by ideas of social transformation and willing to sacrifice the lives of millions to their ideals are not the kinds of leaders that the world needs (then or now). Mantle's difficulty in understanding the play at its simplest level points to the difficulties that any serious new play was going to have on Broadway.

John Anderson in the *New York Journal and American* (25 October 1939) saw the central conflict of the text as being between the God-states of the European dictators and **Buchman's Moral Rearmament**. This catches Dostoevsky's idea of man being put in the place of God and the necessary destruction that follows. While this is to simplify

Buchman and Moral Rearmament: F.N.D. Buchman was a Christian evangelist who founded the Oxford Group in the 1920s. This group believed in the necessity of moral and spiritual renewal based on what they called 'the four absolutes' (absolute honesty, absolute purity, absolute unselfishness, absolute love). This renewal was what was known as Moral Rearmament and in 1938 MRA was established as an international organisation. Alcoholics Anonymous was formed within the Oxford Group in 1934, but by 1939 had separated because they felt that the group was too religious. Also, while, like most people, they saw the importance of the ideals of honesty, purity, unselfishness and love, they felt that putting the word 'absolute' in front put too much emphasis on perfection and that this was driving alcoholics back to drink. Alcoholics Anonymous abandoned religion as such and focused on a more open and inclusive notion of spirituality.

too much, Chekhov was an alcoholic and his renewed spiritual perspective on life followed from him accepting his problem and giving up alcohol. Chekhov, like Dostoevsky, was a devout Christian, if a rather unorthodox one.

DOSTOEVSKY, SOCIALIST REALISM AND BRECHT

Not surprisingly, *The Daily Worker*, an American communist paper, came out strongly against *The Possessed*. This paper aligned itself with the Soviet Union and wouldn't be expected to praise the work of an outcast and 'counter-revolutionary' like Chekhov – remember, Chekhov was considered to be a 'mystic' and therefore a 'sick' artist in Russia when he left in 1928. The state control of the arts and the restrictions on experimentation had increased since Chekhov had left, and **socialist realism** had become the approved mode for art, including performance, in the Soviet Union and for communists and socialists around the world since 1934. Not all of those artists who regarded themselves as communist or left-wing agreed with this position, and perhaps the most notable example of a communist opposed to socialist realism is Bertolt Brecht. Brecht's *Fear and Misery in the Third Reich*, first performed in Paris in 1938, is, like *The Possessed*, written in short scenes and in a non-naturalistic manner. On the other hand, it is more experimental in form than *The Possessed*, because the scenes are more or less free-standing and don't combine to present a single coherent narrative. Furthermore, while both plays engage with violence in contemporary politics, Brecht is attacking fascism while standing on the side of communism. Chekhov and Shdanoff are anti-fascist, recognising the dangers of Hitler and Mussolini, but are also painfully aware of the violence and destruction of the Russian Revolution.

Socialist realism: the approved mode for all art and literature in the Soviet Union from 1934–91. All art was to be rooted in an optimistic and heroic view of the achievements of the Revolution. This perspective was to be represented through a realistic style, which was free from formalist experiments and from the world of the 'impossible'.

Dostoevsky's novel was inspired by the Nechaev affair. Sergei Nechaev (1847–82) was a Russian nihilist and anarchist who believed in violent revolution. In November 1869, Nechaev and three other members of his group arranged a meeting in a Moscow park with a former member of their group, Ivan Ivanov. Ivanov had left the Nechaev circle because he felt that Nechaev was becoming too dictatorial. Nechaev and the others were worried that he might turn informer, so they lured him to the park, beat him unconscious, strangled him, shot him in the head and, just to make sure, dropped his body weighed down with bricks through a hole in the ice covering the lake. In Dostoevsky's first draft of *The Possessed* Verkhovensky is called Nechaev, and Dostoevsky's aim is to warn against the dangers of a destructive nihilism which finds it acceptable to kill people in the interests of an ideal – this is picked up in Shdanoff's text. Again the work of Brecht is worth comparing. Brecht's short 'teaching piece', *The Measures Taken* (1930), is written in short scenes and examines the story of a group of revolutionary agitators who have killed their comrade. The question is: Were they correct to do so? Brecht's argument is that they were and the executed comrade agrees to his own death as being necessary. By getting the character to agree to his death, Brecht avoids the question as to whether or not the killers were morally right. The only question becomes whether or not the killing was justified in terms of the revolution. The agitators acknowledge that 'it is a terrible thing to kill', but at the same time assert that violence is the only way in which the world can be changed. Shdanoff and Chekhov realised that it was this kind of attitude which led to the killing of millions within the Soviet Union. It had almost caused the death of Chekhov himself in 1928, and certainly led to the assassination of Meyerhold and of Zinaida Raikh, his wife, in 1940.

Brecht would have agreed with the denunciation of Chekhov's work as both mystical and counter-revolutionary, but he was also strongly antagonistic to the doctrine of socialist realism. Had he been writing against socialist realism in the Soviet Union, he would have been at risk himself, and it is instructive that, when he was forced to leave Nazi Germany in 1935, he fled to western Europe and then the United States – regions with strong liberal democratic traditions and values. *The Possessed* then, is warning of the dangers of a belief in violent revolution and comes out against the view that it is worth killing fifteen million people for future freedom. In *The Measures Taken* the scale of this revolutionary violence is concealed and it is unclear how many people Brecht thinks it is acceptable to kill in the process of social transformation.

In the light of all of this it is interesting to note that Richard Watts Jr, in the *New York Herald Tribune* (25 October 1939), described the politics of the piece as involving a 'sinister combination of fascism and communism', which was frightening because it appeared that Europe was in the process of devising precisely such an amalgam. Once again there is the failure to see that Chekhov and Shdanoff were trying to avoid the extremes of both fascism and communism. The character of The Stranger, who appears in a scene that doesn't come from Dostoevsky, tells a version of the folk tale 'Ivan the Good', in which Ivan tells the people that he doesn't want to rule over them by force; these are key moments in the play which signal clearly the need for consensual government.

Had Chekhov chosen to present a production of *Twelfth Night* for the school's first showing on Broadway, the critics would doubtless have found it easier to understand and could have enjoyed the performances, rather than worrying about the structure and content of the play. But Chekhov had chosen to produce *The Possessed* precisely because it dealt with the difficult issues of the day. Leaving aside discussions of the text and its content, let's look at how the performances by these young students were received and try to get a sense of the performance style from among the various perceptions of the reviewers.

CASTING

While Chekhov was auditioning new students for the Ridgefield Studio, he was looking for potential actors to play the key roles of Stavrogin and Pyotr Verkhovensky. Unfortunately, there were no obvious choices to play these two major roles and he considered hiring in a couple of professional actors. This would have been quite a difficult thing to do. The actors would still need to be able to work with the Chekhov technique, even if their basic stagecraft was stronger. In the end, however, he decided to work with two of the students, Woodrow Chambliss as Verkhovensky and Blair Cutting as Stavrogin. Beatrice Straight was to play Liza, Hurd Hatfield, Kirilov and Mary Lou Taylor, Martha. By March 1939, however, while he was happy with Chambliss as Verkhovensky, Cutting had been replaced by John Flynn as Stavrogin and took on the role of Shatov. At this stage, Chekhov still felt that it was important that Dorothy Elmhirst came over from Dartington to play Mrs Stavrogin, in order to give some added weight and experience to the cast. In the end it was Ellen van Volkenburg, a professional actress, who took on the role, but Elmhirst had done a considerable amount of work on it with Shdanoff and commented in a letter to Chekhov that she had a difficulty finding the fiery qualities necessary for the role because she was so quiet herself. This difficulty in being able to transform oneself into a character with different qualities from our everyday selves is at the heart of how the Chekhov technique tries to help the actor. Chambliss found it difficult to transform himself from a soft, charming person into Verkhovensky, but Chekhov was surprised with how far he was able to develop some of the necessary qualities. The ability of the student actors to transform themselves convinced him that the technique, by enabling them to work in a continuous manner and not rely on talent, was effective. Chekhov did, however, hire two other professional actors to play relatively minor roles. Despite requests, especially from Dorothy Elmhirst, that he take on a role himself, he refused on two grounds: first, because of his Russian accent and, second, because he considered it impossible to act and direct at the same time.

THE CRITICS AND THE PERFORMANCE

The ensemble

Despite the reviewers' dislike of the script, there were a considerable number of positive responses to the directing and acting, even though they were often heavily qualified. Mason Brown, for example, disliked the script, and found the performance 'somber' and 'appallingly tortured and confused'; yet he notes that the audience followed the performance in silence and attributes this to the talent of the company as performers and to Chekhov's direction.

One of the key aspects of the acting that critics identified was the strength of the ensemble. This was something that was as important to Chekhov as it had been to his teacher Stanislavsky, and the programme included a note affirming that the Chekhov company did not believe in the idea of 'star' performers and regarded all members of the company as equals, regardless of their role. This was, of course, as unusual for a production on Broadway as it would have been in London's West End, where the star culture dominated and still does to a great extent today. Gielgud, in his review of Stanislavsky's *An Actor Prepares*, doubted whether the ensemble method of acting could possibly work in the West End, with its commercialism based on the star system. To push the message home, there were no cast biographies included in the programme.

This commitment to equality on behalf of the players didn't prevent the critics from picking out the individuals who they felt gave the most interesting performances. Of course, this is always going to happen and in any performance some performers are likely to be more successful or have a greater impact that others. The difference between an ensemble and a star vehicle is that, in the latter, the star is always at the centre of the performance and all other actors are only there to support them regardless of the production. An ensemble of the kind represented by the Chekhov company, on the other hand, will have performers who take a leading role in one production and then a smaller one in another no one can assume that any particular part belongs to them. This is something that Chekhov took from Stanislavsky: the idea that there are 'no small parts only small actors'. Beatrice Straight was, perhaps, to take the art of the small part to extremes when she won an Academy Award for the Best Supporting Actress for her role in the movie, *Network* (1976). She was on-screen for under six minutes in a film that was over two hours long and with a cast that included Faye Dunaway, Robert Duvall, William Holden and Peter Finch.

Reviewers of *The Possessed* praised the company for working exceptionally well as an ensemble. Brooks Atkinson in *The New York Times*, however, saw a more sinister dimension to the ensemble work. He described the company as a group of 'muscle-bound actors', who, far from being free and creative artists, performed 'by rote' under the direction of Chekhov, who, he claimed, behaved like a despotic dictator who has destroyed their spirit. Nothing could be further from Chekhov's aims and Atkinson is aware of the irony, at least in relation to the message of the play. Once again, we see a political reading of the play that's at odds with Chekhov's aims. This time the reading doesn't focus on the content of the play, but on the physicality of the actors. It is as though Atkinson reads the physique of the actors as if they are the embodiment of socialist realist sculpture, or as if the very fact of their working as an ensemble implied a loss of individuality.

Nonetheless, in keeping with other reviewers, he identifies the political meeting scene (which was the longest and most complex in the play) as 'brilliant', possessing the 'genius of theatricality' which filled the theatre with 'sound, movement and frenzy'.

Inexperience and excess tension (trying too hard)

There were a number of problems picked out, however, which will have given Chekhov cause for concern. The first was that a number of critics felt that there was too much tension in the performers. Given that a feeling of ease on the stage was of central importance to Chekhov's work, the criticism that the performers were too tense is a significant one – clearly they weren't yet accomplished enough to carry off a performance in front of a Broadway audience. John Mason Brown identified a problem with the concentration of the performers. It wasn't that their concentration was sloppy or weak, but that they spent so much time showing that they were concentrating, with 'bulging eyes' and 'immovable' stares, and also that they were trying too hard to show that they were listening. For Chekhov the performers should be concentrating with a feeling of ease. If Mason Brown's assessment is accurate, then we have further evidence that the actors were suffering from excessive tension and this would inevitably have affected the dynamics of the performance. With excess tension, everything begins to flatten out and the actors lose their sense of flow and of rhythm. Brooks Atkinson in *The New York Times* blames the acting style for killing the spontaneity of the actors; that is, the stiffness and tension isn't seen as a result of the actors' nervousness but as a result of the aesthetic choice made by the director.

Connecting with the audience

Another criticism of the actors came from the reviewer of *The Christian Science Monitor*, who didn't feel that there was enough contact between the audience and the performers. It is unlikely that this is a complaint that there was too little direct address, so it is an interesting criticism, given that the co-creativity of the audience is crucial for Chekhov. None of the reviewers commented on the atmosphere of the piece, perhaps because they lacked the vocabulary, but, if Chekhov's theory that the atmosphere unites the audience and the performance works in practice, the audience should feel engaged even if they can't explain why. On the other hand, Mason Brown's comment that the audience were very quiet during the performance suggests that there was a unifying atmosphere of some kind. It is impossible to know for sure, of course, and the tension in the actors would certainly have affected their ability to build a rapport with an audience. Yet it is important to note that this group of partially trained and inexperienced actors managed to hold the audience – they must have been doing something right!

Characterisation and acting style

Woodrow ('Woody') Chambliss played Pyotr Verkhovensky as a 'super sulphurous slavic Mephistopheles' (John Mason Brown), wearing a brown derby, glasses, large box coat (overcoat) and leather gloves and carrying a small pistol. The costume led some critics to note that Verkhovensky looked like a comic character from Dickens and there was some concern that this was inappropriate in a 'serious' play. One critic caught on that Chekhov saw a 'mischievousness' in Verkhovensky, which made him an almost absurd rather than a conventionally evil villain. Richard Lockridge in *The New York Sun* (25 October 1939) also has a difficulty relating the humour to the piece; for example, he describes Chambliss's Verkhovensky as 'scuttling darkly behind bits of scenery'. This evocative description paints a grotesque image of Verkhovensky, moving with short, hasty steps. If I let my imagination go into this, I get an image of a beetle and think of the story 'Metamorphosis' by **Franz Kafka** (in which Gregor Samsa awakes to find himself transformed into a gigantic insect) and the subsequent physical theatre adaptation by **Steven Berkoff**. Whether or not my image of a beetle here is strictly accurate, we can see that, if we're trying to view Chambliss's performance through a naturalistic lens, to assess how 'true to life' it is on a surface level, we'll fail to grasp what's happening. If we read Lockridge's description as accurate, but put his judgement to one side, this appears to be an example of the fantastic realism that Chekhov took from Vakhtangov – a style which incorporates the use of the grotesque.

We can take this further by picking up on the reference to Dickens. Chekhov's admiration for Dickens is well established and his initial objective was to produce *The Possessed* and *Pickwick* simultaneously. Perhaps less well known is Dostoevsky's admiration of Dickens and, in particular, the character of Samuel Pickwick. The two are linked together by their use of exaggeration and the grotesque, although with quite different qualities. Verkhovensky is the chief villain in *The Possessed* and argues that 'freedom is an illusion . . . individuality is a lie' and for the importance of 'racial blood'. In this sense he embodies the 'sinister combination of communism and fascism' that Richard Watts seemed to apply to the whole play. But Chekhov, like Stanislavsky, doesn't want us to see Verkhovensky as completely evil, but as a human being possessed by a destructive idea. The kind of humour to be found in Dickens lightens the representation of Verkhovensky and adds another dimension to the performance. Had Chekhov been able to produce *The Possessed* and *Pickwick* at the same time, then critics might have been able to see the correspondences in style between the two; instead, a number of them found it difficult to understand the style. Lockridge, for example, felt that Verkhovensky's movement around the space became 'funny', but doesn't consider whether or not the humour is part of the characterisation. If we bring back the idea of mischievousness and add to it the image of scuttling darkly, we begin to get a sense of character that's not contained in one description alone.

Hurd Hatfield's Kirilov, a character who plans to commit suicide to further the cause of the revolution, was angular and slightly camp, with a centre parting. Lockridge described him as an 'awesome character', who spends the first eleven scenes staring straight ahead and then shoots himself. This conjures up a strong image that suggests that Kirilov has no other function in the play. In fact, before he kills himself he betrays

Figure 3.1 *The Possessed* (October 1939): Hurd Hatfield as Kirilov

Shatov (Blair Cutting), who is killed by Verkhovensky and his cronies. When Lockridge writes that Kirilov is 'comical right from the start', it's not clear whether he finds the characterisation ridiculous; that is, whether he finds it difficult to accept the character or is picking up a sense of humour that, as with Verkhovensky, Chekhov would want to be there as a balance to the intense seriousness.

Other performers received reviews which tell us very little about their presence onstage. Beatrice Straight, for example, is praised for a moment of 'dark beauty and terror', when she realises that the man she loves is nothing more than an 'empty husk' (*Theatre Arts Monthly*, December 1939: 858). This doesn't give us an overall sense of her characterisation, although it does tell us something of the power of her performance. John Flynn, playing Stavrogin, dilated his eyes with 'monotonous frequency', according to the critic of *Women's Wear Daily* (25 October 1939) and, while this hints at a grotesque characterisation, it really isn't enough to go on.

I've been claiming that the critics were somewhat confused about the style of work for which Chekhov was aiming and this sense of misunderstanding is heightened by the praise given to Ellen van Volkenburg. Playing Mrs Stavrogin, the role she took over from Dorothy Elmhirst, van Volkenburg was considered to be the only actor to create a character who was close to being human being. I take from this that there was a critical assumption that the characters should appear to be human beings; that is, human beings behaving in a naturalistic, everyday manner. That van Volkenburg should get such praise is interesting, as she joined the cast late on and wasn't even as experienced in Chekhov's methods as the members of the school. Without being able to see a recording of the performance, it is difficult to assess exactly what the critics were seeing. But, as we begin to put together the various comments, it does seem as though the critics were in favour of a naturalistic performance and used the term 'grotesque' as a negative term rather than appreciating that this was very much part of Chekhov's style. The critic of *The Sunday Times* (29 October 1939), for example, considered that the piece was directed in a 'bizarre style of Russian madness'.

The reviewer in *The Daily Worker* attacked the cast for 'overacting' and said that the actors' 'postures, struttings, leaps and bounds make Dostoevsky seem like a marijuana addict's dream' (26 October 1939). Once again, through the negative criticism we can get a glimpse of

Figure 3.2 *The Possessed* (October 1939): John Flynn as Stavrogin and Ellen van Volkenburg as Mrs Stavrogin

something else. If the critic was wanting a piece of socialist realism, with a naturalistic acting style, then Chekhov's actors were bound to seem as if they were 'overacting'. The reference to an 'addict's dream' gives further evidence that the piece was in a non-naturalistic style and that the reviewer found this difficult. It is interesting that the strong physicality of the actors, their 'postures, struttings, leaps and bounds', should produce this effect on the communist critic. It suggests a chaotic performance which lacked discipline. On the other hand, we've seen that another critic, Atkinson, also drew attention to the physicality of the actors and used it as evidence for an excess of discipline. The common ground of these two critics is their recognition of the significance of a stylised physicality. They each have a difficulty relating to this physicality. Lockridge also had a difficulty with the physical style of performance, but he connected it to the intense pace of the action. He saw that the theme of the play was important and relevant to what was happening in the world at the time and ought to wake the audience up. Instead of being woken up, however, he felt that the style of the piece was battering the audience into semi-consciousness. He felt there was insufficient control of the play's dynamics with fifteen scenes of 'angry dialogue', and with the company acting 'furiously' and without a 'pause for breath'. Given the importance of the pause for Chekhov, this is quite surprising. Was it the sheer physicality and intensity of the performance that was disturbing? Or is there other evidence to suggest that the problem was a lack of directorial control over the dynamics of the performance?

The dynamics of the production

Chekhov, like any director, was held responsible for the overall dynamics of the piece. For the reviewer in *Theatre Arts Monthly* (December 1939: 857–8), key criticisms were that the performance was overstrained and overdramatic, that it was 'keyed' too high from the beginning and that there was no gradation in the direction. In this sense, it was felt that the audience didn't have time to get into the style of the performance. It was noted that the performance worked best in the 'quieter' scenes, but that there were too few moments of stillness. The mention of 'quieter' scenes indicates that *The Possessed* wasn't performed at a continuously furious pace and that there was at least some variation; and, while the reviewer considers that there was too little stillness, there were at least some moments when the action slowed right down. So, while the overall impression is of an intense physical performance with a blistering pace and loud vocalisation, there are contrasting moments of quietness and stillness. The sense that the performance was 'overstrained' was a more subtle criticism than one which claimed that the actors were overacting. 'Overstrained' suggests that the actors were pushing at their limits and, as the reviewer points out, when a climax might have been reached the actors had nowhere to go and had exhausted their vocabulary. This hints once again at the inexperience of actors who had not yet mastered their art and suggests that the director, by keying the performance too high, was asking too much of them.

Chekhov saw *The Possessed* as being 'near to tragedy' and wanted the audience to be frightened by it. He saw it as a 'form full of content and ready to break' – this gives us a sense that there was an attempt to signal in the performance that it was the form itself that was 'overstrained' and close to breaking point. Still, we have to return to the fact that, although the form might be overstrained, the actors still needed to communicate this with a sense of lightness and ease, and this doesn't appear to have been the case.

The reviewer in *Theatre Arts Monthly* also described the play as consisting of fifteen scenes of 'extreme violence and tension', which were as 'exhausting to watch as they must have been to perform'. Yet the same reviewer had earlier in the piece described the performance as 'an arresting example of directorial virtuosity'. In what sense could Chekhov's direction of *The Possessed* be described as virtuosic and arresting, while at the same time lacking an appropriate command of theatrical dynamics? Shouldn't the two be mutually exclusive? Certainly the reviewer signed off by claiming that there was too little variation in acting styles on the Broadway stage, as well as too little experimentation and boldness in direction, and praised the company for its risk-taking. Arthur Pollock in *The Brooklyn Eagle* (25 October 1939) considered that Chekhov had staged the play with 'remarkable suppleness', which, if we add the idea of 'directorial virtuosity', seems to suggest that there was a sense of rhythm and a controlled dynamic in the production, even if this was marred at times by the cast's nervousness and inexperience. Pollock wrote that *The Possessed* was 'something special, something unlike anything to be seen in New York at the moment'.

Praising the detail

This discussion of the overall style and dynamic of the performance and the possible lack of control by the performers might lead us to expect that the individual performances were not quite up to scratch for a Broadway performance, even if the ensemble work was of a high quality. This would be a mistake. The detailed characterisation which was achieved was praised by John Mason Brown, who identified the small gestures that fitted perfectly with the character and that were at a level not even dreamed of by most American companies. This is high praise for a company which is making its first public showing and who are still, at this point, a student group. The physical and vocal discipline of the performers was also praised by reviewers. It is important to bear this in mind when reading evaluations of Chekhov's work during this period.

The design

The stage and costume designs were by Mstislav Dobuzhinsky (1875–1957), who designed *A Month in the Country* for Stanislavsky at the Moscow Arts Theatre as well as designing for Diaghilev's Ballets Russes. Dobuzhinsky's set for *The Possessed* consisted of a series of small inset stages against black hangings, with window and sky effects projected on to a backdrop. It was clearly not a set for a naturalistic production and it had an expressionistic feel that was very much in keeping with the sense of fantastic realism and the grotesque that I've been trying to tease out. The set was viewed positively by most critics, although there was some criticism that it created difficulties for the actors, with the action seeming too crowded at times. A difficulty here is that it's not possible to know whether the overcrowded moments were an accidental consequence of the design or part of Chekhov's conception.

Lost humour

We've seen how some critics found it difficult to cope with the production and were unable to find a way of relating to the humour that was implicit in Chekhov's vision of the grotesque. Perhaps part of their difficulty was their stereotyped image of Russian culture.

Figure 3.3
The Possessed (October 1939): Woodrow Chambliss as Verkhovensky and John Flynn as Stavrogin

Sidney B. Whipple, for example, used his review in the *World Telegram* (31 October 1939) to attack Russian culture in general. He described Russians as a 'sour, gloomy and hopeless race', and weighed into Anton Chekhov's *Three Sisters* as an example of this, giving the impression that the American stage would be better off without these imports. As for the Chekhov company, he didn't think that there was a place for them on Broadway.

In spite of his derogatory remarks about Russians, Whipple did, however, make an important observation. He remarked that there was a loss of humour in the adaptation from Dostoevsky, whose writings, particularly *The Possessed*, he considered to be full of grotesque humour. Whipple was not alone in this view – John D. Beaufort in *The Christian Science Monitor* (25 October 1939) also commented that there were too few traces of humour in the production. There is very little, if any, overt humour in Shdanoff's script, but Chekhov's own emphasis on the importance of humour makes this lack surprising. Perhaps the problem here is that the lack of ease in the performance meant that the sense of openness and warmth that accompanies humour was restricted. This might explain why some critics were unsure whether some moments were supposed to be humorous in such a 'serious' play, while others, like Whipple and Beaufort, clearly felt the humour should have been there but wasn't. On the other hand, Whipple is as inconsistent in his remarks as some of the other critics. He finds the costume comical, for example, but doesn't make the connection to the humour he feels is lacking. What seems to be going on is that the critics are focusing on the script without exploring the relationship between the text and the action and how one comments upon the other.

SUMMING UP

What does all of this add up to? *An exciting piece of physical theatre with detailed characterisation, performed in a style which was not fully grasped by the Broadway critics*. There were some weaknesses in the overall control of the performance, which affected the performance dynamics, but this was a surprisingly accomplished performance by a young company. There might have been some uncertainty as to the wisdom of the choice of text for an initial Broadway performance, but Chekhov's approach to training and directing was relatively successful in artistic terms. The lack of critical understanding of what Chekhov was trying to achieve meant that the reviews came down mostly on what were perceived as the negative aspects of the production and *The Possessed* was a commercial failure.

Chekhov was very disappointed in the reception of *The Possessed*; he was prepared for negative criticism, but he was 'crushed and depressed' by the 'plain, banal, huge and shameless dishonesty' of the criticism. By exploring the critical response and attempting to get a sense of the performance from both the positive and negative criticisms, we can see that it might be more a case of a lack of understanding rather than dishonesty. The critics weren't equipped to deal effectively with what Chekhov was trying to do in *The Possessed*, but they were sharp enough to realise that it didn't quite work, even though it had many admirable qualities.

TWELFTH NIGHT (1940)

After the financial disaster of *The Possessed*, Chekhov abandoned his production of *Pickwick* and turned towards two works with which he'd already had success: Shakespeare's *Twelfth Night* (with the Habima) and an adaptation of Dickens' *The Cricket on the Hearth* (with the MAT). These two productions toured New England and some southern states, playing in university theatres and community centres.

Chekhov felt that the group made 'great strides' and the critical reception of *Twelfth Night* was very positive. Reviewers picked out the production's rhythm, music, harmony and unbroken line. One perceptive writer praised the company's 'joyous and vibrant theatricality', which, he suggested, simultaneously reminded a twentieth-century audience of the 'Ballets Russes and Walt Disney's cartoons'. This suggests precisely the combination of precision and fun that Chekhov admired in Vakhtangov and that was somehow missing from *The Possessed*. There was a strong sense of connection between performer and audience, which critics had also pointed out as lacking in the earlier production. In contrast to the inexperienced group who had appeared in *The Possessed*, the critics now saw a young group who showed a 'maturity beyond their years'.

Chekhov felt that Shakespeare should be edited and rearranged if necessary, to make the plays more suited to the times. *Twelfth Night* was cut from five acts to two plus a prologue, which inevitably sped up the action. The scene changes were done in full view of the audience by members of the cast in period costume, and the tempo of the changes was suited to the mood of the action. This suggests that the actors performing the scene change were effecting a change in atmosphere as much as a change in the arrangement of objects in space. In other words, the scene changes were *psychophysical actions*.

The set was designed by Chekhov, and was appropriately portable for a touring production. It consisted of reversible curtains, a turntable throne, miniature trees made out of coloured wood and a portable door frame and door with an attached balcony. The sense of portability, necessary for a touring production, was woven into the texture of the performance itself with the rhythmic scene changes.

One reviewer, who had the opportunity to observe the company in rehearsal, described Chekhov as a 'quiet-mannered' director who 'understands' the actors' problems and 'gently suggests slight changes' (*Albany Times*, 16 October 1940). This is quite a contrast from the kind of director that appears to have been imagined by the critics of *The Possessed*.

Chekhov's production of *Twelfth Night*, which was also to be well received on Broadway, appears to have improved on much of what was wrong with *The Possessed*. The overall sense was of an ensemble per-formance that was vibrantly physical, vocally clear, swift moving, imaginative, well characterised and superbly directed. There had been tremendous progress in the ensemble from the first production, but the qualities that were evident in *Twelfth Night* were also there in *The Possessed*. The difference in reception appears to have been partly to do with the intense reaction to the style and subject matter of *The Possessed*. In both productions we can see that Chekhov's approach to training was having a powerful effect on his students. It may be the case that they were exposed too soon on the Broadway stage, but we have seen that, even at that formative stage, they were producing high-quality performances. In simple terms, Chekhov's approach to actor training was working.

PICKWICK

Although there isn't a stage production of *Pickwick* to discuss, it's worth taking some time to look at Chekhov's and Henry Lyon Young's script and at Chekhov's rehearsal notes, to get some insight as to how Chekhov was working at the time of *The Possessed*. Charles Dickens' *The*

Pickwick Papers (1836–7) is a novel that stretches to over 800 pages and would obviously need considerable cutting to be brought to a manageable size for the stage.

SYNOPSIS OF SCENE ONE

The opening scene sees Samuel Pickwick announcing to the Pickwick Club that he is about to undertake a journey of discovery with three of his colleagues: Tupman, Snodgrass and Winkle. In the next room Pickwick's landlady, Mrs Bardell, and her friend, Mrs Cluppins, have paused in the process of drinking their tea to listen to what's happening, while Mrs Bardell's son, Tommy, is spying through the keyhole. At the end of the meeting, Pickwick sees off his guests and Mrs Bardell and Mrs Cluppins have a brief conversation, which is interrupted by Sam Weller who's come to see Pickwick. When Pickwick returns, he calls Mrs Bardell to his room with the intention of informing her that he's appointing a new manservant, Sam. With Sam waiting outside, and Mrs Cluppins and Tommy listening at the door, Pickwick's rather indirect words are misunderstood by Mrs Bardell, who thinks that he's proposing marriage. She's so overcome with excitement that she faints into his arms. Tommy, not understanding at all, thinks that Pickwick is attacking his mother and springs to her defence, bursting into the room with Mrs Cluppins and Snodgrass, Tupman and Winkle, who have just arrived. Mrs Bardell, in a state of great happiness, is led back to her room, while Pickwick tries to explain what happened to his friends – not having realised that Mrs Bardell thinks that he's proposed to her. Overhearing the conversation, Mrs Bardell and Mrs Cluppins realise that Pickwick has no intention of honouring the proposal, the one very distressed and the other very angry. Meanwhile, Sam has his interview with Pickwick, they agree the terms of the employment and the group sets out for Rochester. Mrs Cluppins goes out to come back with a solicitor, Mr Fogg, and the legal process, which will end in Pickwick's imprisonment for breach of promise, gets under way.

There's quite a lot of action in this short scene, which brings together material that is separated by nearly 200 pages in the novel. Each of the sequences in the novel is considerably longer than the whole scene here, but they are reduced to their essential actions and placed alongside each other. This gives a very clear exposition of the conflict that is at the heart of the novel, but that takes hundreds of pages to take shape. Someone with less experience of adaptation and of the processes of making theatre would create a much more linear text. While they are aware that cuts will be necessary, both in the story and in the dialogue, they won't think to take different scenes from different parts of the story and put them together in order to clarify the major themes.

Making use of the possibility of two related actions occurring simultaneously on the stage, Chekhov and Lyons create a scene that cuts rhythmically between the two rooms, which might as well be two different worlds when it comes to the inhabitants of each room understanding the others' language.

CHEKHOV'S NOTES ON THE SCENE

In his director's notes for the unstaged *Pickwick*, Chekhov gives clear indication for character, including objectives and inner gestures. The first thing he notes is that we are entering something which is already in process, a moment of change for the Pickwick Club. Because Pickwick is announcing a new adventure, there is a sense of openness, of expansion in the room. By way of contrast, in Mrs Bardell's room there is a sense of contraction. Why is this? Because the occupants of Mrs Bardell's room are spying, they are engaging in a covert, closed activity. They are drawing information into themselves and not giving anything out. Chekhov suggests that the actors see these opposites of expansion and contraction as gestures. We looked at archetypal gestures of expansion and contraction in the previous section, where we had a sense of the action extending out beyond the body. We then considered this in relation to the Psychological Gesture. What Chekhov is asking the actor to do here is to imagine that there is a gesture for the whole room. When I begin to imagine this, I see a large figure in each room, of which all the characters are a part. In one room this large figure is expanding and carrying all the characters with it; in the other room the figure is contracting. In this way I get a sense of all of the characters being a part of something larger than themselves. There are many different ways of imagining this and there is no right or wrong way, as long as you get the sense of the scene in each room having a particular gesture.

This doesn't mean that, onstage, all of the people in one room will be making large, expansive gestures, but that they are part of an expansive atmosphere. Chekhov suggests that the atmosphere in Pickwick's room is that of a 'light, sunny day' together with a sense of 'celebration'.

CHEKHOV'S NOTES ON THE CHARACTERS

Pickwick

This sense of celebration is particularly attached to Pickwick, who keeps his sunny disposition throughout most of the scene, only ruffled when Mrs Bardell approaches him too intimately. Chekhov sees Pickwick as having a quality of 'showing off', coupled with a 'tremendous power of radiation' and large and expansive gestures. His face is quite open and it is very difficult for him to conceal anything from those around him. In fact, it doesn't occur to him to hide anything, because he is wonderfully naive. He is a man who knows that others look at him and who recognises that he is charming and well dressed. Throughout the scene Pickwick has an inner gesture of 'flying up, then down, then up'. Chekhov describes this as a kind of 'buoyancy' and connects it to a 'quality of lifting himself up like a bouncing ball'.

These physical and psychological qualities are also reflected in Chekhov's conception of Pickwick's speech. Pickwick shows off as much in his speech as in his action and he 'loves to make forms and shapes with his speech'. At this moment Chekhov doesn't discuss the kinds of forms that Pickwick likes to make, but we can see how he does this with his consideration of Mrs Bardell.

Mrs Bardell

The notes on Mrs Bardell, for example, are perhaps even more detailed than they are for Pickwick. Chekhov offers the image that she forms her words 'like little dumplings . . . little tasty things'. This is a more specific sense of vocal form than Chekhov has given for Pickwick, but perhaps that in itself is an indication of character. Pickwick is showing off, so enjoys playing with form, whereas Mrs Bardell is less conscious of the forms she makes (although the actor, of course, needs to be very clear about the vocal form as an aspect of characterisation).

Let's look at Chekhov's conception of Mrs Bardell in a little more detail. She is 'flowing like a liquid – always giving herself to everything and everyone' and this is made even more complex:

> When she is listening she is flowing – everything is enveloped in this watery flowing.

And:

> A movement like waves – like a boat – soaring, gliding – coming down she is accepting everything, going up she is embracing everything. Quick psychological power moving very slowly.
>
> (Chekhov 1939)

At the beginning of the scene she is listening to everything with a sense of hope, as if it were a 'sermon from Heaven', and then, towards the end of the scene, when she has realised that Pickwick isn't going to marry her after all, she 'falls into a bottomless abyss into which she goes deeper and deeper'. Her Psychological Gesture is 'to receive everything', which is linked to the fact of her 'quietly accepting her destiny'. We can see how this is there, first in her acceptance that Pickwick wants to marry her, then in her acceptance that he doesn't and, finally, in her acceptance of Mrs Cluppins bringing the solicitor. In fact, Chekhov notes that Mrs Cluppins' influence over Mrs Bardell is so great that she acts like a filter between her friend and the world.

Mrs Cluppins

Mrs Cluppins is perhaps the character who provides the strongest contrast to Pickwick in Chekhov's conception of this opening scene. While Pickwick is expansive and drawing attention to himself through his showing off, Mrs Cluppins is 'contracting everything'. She is like a 'lobster' or a 'crab' who is constantly on the look out for 'victims' who she can snatch with her claws. But in their polarities of expansion and contraction, Pickwick and Mrs Cluppins are joined by the fact that they both need to be the centre of attention and pay little heed to the needs of others.

In this discussion of the characters, we can see Chekhov bringing together different aspects of the training into quite complex characterisations, and he does this with the other characters in the scene as well. The level of detail here is quite difficult to absorb, and Chekhov's notes continue in this vein for the whole of the play. There is a huge amount of information for the actor who's going to be playing the character, but there is also considerable space for their own creativity. A consideration of these notes gives us a sense of the kind of direction Chekhov offered to his actors during this period and we can imagine this level of information being given to actors during *The Possessed*.

SOME THOUGHTS ON THE REHEARSAL PROCESS

During *The Possessed*, Chekhov did have his actors rehearse scenes in their own words (Byckling 1995: 34), and we can also imagine explorations that would involve playing the scene without words, just with the actions and inner gestures. Atmosphere was so important to Chekhov that we can imagine him exploring them with the actors for each scene and ensuring that everything fitted together. Because there is such a clear sense of group atmosphere and inner gesture in the opening scene of Pickwick, perhaps he would have had the actors construct group sculptures for each atmosphere. Because we don't have a detailed record of the rehearsal process for *The Possessed* and the work on *Pickwick* wasn't developed into performance, we don't know for certain exactly which exercises were used to achieve Chekhov's aims. We can, however, have a sense of the *kinds* of exercises he used and use our imaginations. Deirdre Hurst du Prey published a sample of four classes from July, August and September 1939 that are useful in this respect. The two July classes deal with exercises in the feelings of ease, form, beauty and the whole, although the tone of the class suggests that it wasn't for his regular students. The August class focuses on the rehearsal of some scenes from *Pickwick*; one scene in particular has a quality of 'raging nature' (du Prey 1978: 25) and, as we might guess, one of the basic exercises is used:

> Imagine the air around you filled with the atmosphere – filled with this raging thing around you. Don't try to squeeze anything out of yourselves – that would be wrong. Everything is in tremendous movement, in you and around you. If you will imagine this raging atmosphere truly, you will become either as small as a mouse or as big as King Lear. You will merge with it.
>
> (ibid.)

Chekhov then goes on to give instructions which tell the actors how each character responds to this atmosphere. The whole scene is tightly scored in terms of atmospheres and each character's response to the atmosphere is proposed. There is consideration of how scenes fit together and the relationship between them in terms of rhythm. In addition to this, there is consideration of the psychological gesture, as we saw in the notes for the first scene.

In the notes to *The Government Inspector* (Leonard 1984), Chekhov offers a detailed vision of action and characterisation which is quite different from his notes to *Pickwick*. There is clear scoring of atmospheres, marking what the dominant atmosphere is in each section of the play and where it changes into the next, which is also to be found in the notes to *Pickwick*. However, the notes on the characters are far more external. There is nothing to compare with the description of inner gestures of radiating, flying or flowing, or the images we have seen that Chekhov links to these. The notes to *The Government Inspector* aren't written for a group of actors trained in Chekhov's technique, so there is nothing about the psychological gesture. Here is a brief example which gives a flavour of the difference:

> Artemy's fear and despair about the conditions in his hospital raise his voice in pitch and volume, drawing Anton's attention back to the group still at the door.
>
> (Leonard 1963: 143)

The feelings of the character are clear (fear and despair), as is the cause of the feelings (conditions in hospital), the effect of feelings on his voice (rises in pitch and volume), and the effect of his voice on the other character (draws his attention to the group at the door). But there is no indication as to how the actor might access all of this.

In respect of the score of atmospheres in *The Government Inspector*, Chekhov is very precise. He recommends that the actors all mark their scripts with the atmospheres and where they change, and suggests that the work on the play starts with establishing the first atmosphere. The actors should create the atmosphere, not yet worrying about characterisation, and move in harmony with it. Once they've begun to get a sense of the atmosphere in this way they should take a line from the text and try to speak it in harmony with the atmosphere. The director should be looking out for the vocal tone, to check whether it sounds in keeping with the atmosphere or not. The next development is to check that both vocal tone and movement quality are in harmony with the atmosphere (Leonard 1984: 115–17). Taking these suggestions, and information from Chekhov's other writings, we can imagine this kind of exercise being used during the process of rehearsing *The Possessed*, *Twelfth Night*, *The Cricket on the Hearth* and *King Lear*.

4

PRACTICAL
EXERCISES

INTRODUCTION

Well over 100 of Michael Chekhov's exercises have been published, but the technique isn't exhausted by these. Chekhov was inventing new exercises until his death and the basic principles of the technique will allow as many variations and creations as there are creative individualities. What follows is a personal selection of exercises, some previously unpublished, which I've put into my own words. I've taken them from many sources – some from Chekhov's published works, others from classes taught by his students and their students (see Acknowledgements on p. xi).

Which exercises should we do first? There are so many. Chekhov wrote:

> start with the exercises which first appeal to the actor – working conscientiously
> will inevitably lead to the others – organically.
>
> (Chekhov 1942: 279)

Any exercise will reveal what else needs to be learned. If, for example, we started with exercises in 'moulding' and discovered that we had a tendency to tense up our muscles, it would be a signal that we needed to pay more attention to a sense of ease. On the other hand, Chekhov also indicated that it was better to start with the simplest exercises first!

The exercises in this chapter can be followed in sequence or re-organised according to need. Taking just one exercise from each section will give a good taster session. The first one or two exercises in each section are relatively easy, but the work gets more complex as the section goes on.

Sometimes it will be important at a later stage to return to an exercise you've done early on. It's very important not to hold on to an attitude that says 'I've done this exercise so I know it and don't need to do it again.' No matter how many times we've done an exercise, we can always learn more from it. We can satisfy our need for originality and 'newness' by looking for new things in the exercise. By setting ourselves more refined goals within the task, we can improve our skills while keeping ourselves engaged.

One way in which we try to be creative when doing an exercise we've 'done' before is to change the exercise itself rather than just bringing more detail and focus to the task. Sometimes we might not even notice that we're doing it, so the first step is to become aware that we're not doing the task as indicated, but something else, and to notice the difference. Creating new exercises and exploring them is a wonderful thing to do, but it's useful to be aware of whether we're doing this just to avoid the task. Chekhov suggested that we shouldn't invent new exercises until we've mastered the ones set. When we begin to train, there is often a first flush of enthusiasm which wanes as we start to encounter our personal limitations – we might experience this as a lack of spontaneity. Chekhov recognised that this could happen and advised teachers of his technique not to try to find something that's 'more inter-esting' for the student at this point. He was aware that the students might become 'bored and angry' (2000: 16), but that it was a phase that had to be gone through as a part of the process of learning to learn.

There are times when it seems too difficult for us to undertake certain exercises and we need to pay attention to the signals we receive from ourselves. In these instances, however, it is also useful to see if there are ways in which we can participate in the exercise, rather than just opting out.

RESOURCES

Most exercises here assume that you are working as part of a group and have access to a rehearsal space. In my imagination the room is large enough for the whole group to stand in a circle holding hands, to move backwards until your arms are stretched and you are only connected by fingertips, and to allow you to each take three or four steps backwards. You can do most of these exercises in a smaller space and many can be done on your own should you so wish.

Apart from that, you need enough tennis balls, sticks (about a metre in length) and scarves for each person in the group and an easily accessible sound system. That said, most exercises rely solely on the actor's body and imagination.

I haven't made any adjustments to the exercises for groups with significant mobility or sensory differences. Adjustments can be made according to the needs of the group.

ATTITUDE

Chekhov wanted there to be an attitude of warmth, friendliness, freedom and ease in the workspace. Giving and receiving, underpinned by a sense of joy, is at the heart of the work. If we don't find any joy in our work, why do we do it?

Sometimes we need the feedback of others to enable us to become aware of what it is we're doing or not doing, but Chekhov wanted students to avoid giving destructive criticism. One way in which Chekhov used to give feedback was to say: 'That's good! To my mind you achieved x, next time see if you can add y.' The aim here is to praise what has been achieved and to encourage the person to improve. Destructive criticism discourages the person – 'That's crap! You didn't do y' – and contributes to a climate of fear and conflict in the workspace.

We need to develop a mutually supportive atmosphere in this work and some of the exercises will help with that, but we need to keep in mind the effect that our language can have on each other. Being supportive of each other means encouraging each other to participate fully in the work, not colluding in avoiding the task. If we're having a conversation about what we did the night before, then we're clearly not supporting the work. We need to be committed to the work and have an image of ourselves as active, free and energised.

With this in mind, the first few exercises are concerned with arriving in the space and preparing to work with each other.

CROSSING THE THRESHOLD

Chekhov developed an exercise called Crossing the Threshold in order to mark the actor's transition from the world of the everyday into the creative space of the theatre. At its simplest, Crossing the Threshold involves the actor entering the workspace and leaving outside the cares and worries of daily life in order to be ready to work. Troubles can be picked up again at the end of the session if necessary, as the theatre isn't the space for working out personal difficulties. Chekhov's exercises do have great potential for use in therapeutic contexts, but the focus here is on theatre not therapy.

Remember: all exercises are *psychophysical* in Chekhov's approach. Merely stepping backwards and forwards over a line on the floor will produce nothing. Our imaginations must be engaged for these exercises to be effective.

Exercise 4.1

➤   Before crossing the threshold into the workspace, make an inner gesture of leaving your private life behind. Use whatever image comes to you. Perhaps you put your concerns into a box, or bury them under a tree, or maybe you have a gesture of shrugging them off, or pushing them away. Choose whatever works for you, knowing that you can return to them when you leave the class if you need to. You can repeat this inner gesture at any time during the work if new concerns arise or the old ones return.

➤   Imagine a boundary which separates everyday space from the space of the imagination. The boundary can be indicated by a pre-existing line on the floor, or one can be drawn. It isn't necessary to have a 'real' line at all, as long as everyone is clear where the boundary lies. Imagine that the space on the other side of the boundary is your individual creative space, which will nourish and feed your creativity. Step across the boundary and allow yourself to experience this creative space and to sense its possibilities. Make friends with your space. Initially step just across the boundary for a few seconds and allow yourself to sense the difference and then return. Gradually increase the amount of time you spend in the space as you grow in confidence. You are not performing for an audience, there is no script to remember and there is no action to get right. It's your creative space – allow yourself to respond to ideas that arise. Be aware of other people in the space, but at this stage don't interact with them. Retreat across the boundary when you are ready, or when you lose the sense of creativity and freedom.

MAKING CONTACT

Chekhov commented that we were afraid of ourselves and of each other and that this wasn't a good basis on which to develop our creative potential or to make theatre. The exercises in this section and the following one aim to make us feel more at ease with each other and to help in the construction of a supportive atmosphere and in building self-confidence.

Exercise 4.2

➤ The group should stand in a circle holding hands, each person looking around the circle, becoming aware of everyone else who's there. This is done with an attitude of opening oneself to each of the others, so that you are willing to give to and receive from each other in a friendly way. Notice if you have negative feelings towards individuals in the group and gently put them aside; they don't belong in this work. Be aware also of the form of the circle that links you. When a sense of contact has been established, release hands, but keep a sense of the contact and the circle.

➤ Imagine a large golden hoop lying at your feet inside the circle. From the sense of contact, the group should squat down together and lift the hoop in unison, pausing about chest height, and then stretching to send the hoop up into the sky. When you reach the physical limit of your stretch upwards, carry on in your imagination and visualise the hoop going through the roof and disappearing into a clear sky. The group can then sense the moment to lower arms.

➤ The group should find the moment to sit on the floor.

➤ Let the group choose a variety of actions (e.g. jumping three times in the air, quickly touching all four walls of the room, sitting on the floor, standing still or shouting nonsense loudly). Without planning, and keeping a sense of openness and contact, the group should try to sense which action to do as a whole. Perhaps it will run, then shout, then sit, then run again – each person should attempt to sense what's going to happen next.

➤ Try putting a pause after each action, so that the following one always emerges out of stillness.

➤ Try with each action emerging from the previous one without a pause.

➤ Find a partner and stand facing each other. Open yourselves to each other and send out feelings of warmth and acceptance. Once you feel a good connection, begin to move slowly together. No one leads. Try to let the movement arise out of the connection. Don't try to copy each other, but allow your movements to be a response to each other and to grow out of the relationship between you.

➤ Try the same exercise in groups of four, then six, then eight. Then try it with the whole group.

➤ With a new partner, move around the room throwing an imaginary ball to each other. Keep a sense of contact with your partner, whatever your spatial relationship. Try to feel that sense of contact with your whole body – contact is more than just keeping your partner in view. Allow the tempo and rhythm to change and develop, emerging from the interaction between you. Find a moment to come to a stop, but keep the sense of contact.

➤ Do the exercise, but keep a sense of contact with the rest of the group while having your main focus on your partner. The whole group makes the decision to stop.

➤ At the end of the exercise, see if you notice any difference in yourself, or in your relation to your partner or to the whole group?

Chekhov suggested that we need to keep this sense of contact in performance, even when we're offstage. If we stay in touch with our partners, we'll enter the scene at the correct tempo. But we can also have this sense of contact with the set, props and audience.

CONFIDENCE

Chekhov thought that whatever the actor did onstage had to be done with a feeling of confidence and a sense of it being 'well done'. After the performance we can go over what we did and see whether or not we achieved what we were aiming for. Then we can make any changes we need to make for future performances. Whatever we do in the moment of performance, however, is perfect – even our mistakes (and those of our colleagues). Some of us have a critical voice inside us – a devil, Chekhov called it – which is continually telling us that what we do is no good. These exercises are one way of getting that voice to be quiet for a little while.

Exercise 4.3

➤ Throw any object from one hand to the other with a feeling of it being 'well done'. You can always develop what you've done in the future. But, whatever you do, whenever you do it, Chekhov thought that it needed to be done with this sense of being 'well done'. Don't apologise for your presence (your character might do this, but not you as an actor).

➤ The group should form a circle and, one at a time, each member should cross the threshold into the centre of the group. When you are in the centre, whatever you do is perfect. You can make no mistakes. Feel the positive energy coming to you from the audience. Keep a sense of contact with each person in the group. When you are an audience member, try to open yourself to receive the 'performance'.

➤ In front of your audience, juggle with as few or as many objects as you wish. Do everything with a sense of ease. Take risks. Whatever you do is perfect. Keep the sense of it being well done. Try to welcome your 'mistakes' as gifts – they are also 'well done'. See if you can repeat them; do them intentionally. Give your performance a clear, bold ending.

➤ Can you imagine a 'you' who is strong, beautiful, generous, joyful and open? A 'you' who is a creative and skilful performer? Can you get a sense of what that would be like? Try to see it in your imagination and then step into it. If it seems difficult to step into this imaginary 'you' all at once, start with a part, perhaps your hands, first. This might take quite a bit of practice!

➤ Step across the threshold into the circle. Open your arms, sense the centre in your chest and say 'I am (your name). I am an actor.' Leave a pause for your audience to receive your words, then return to your place in the circle. Try to keep the sense of this being an action 'well done'. If you find this difficult, see if you can put the difficulty aside for a moment – you can always return to it later and try again.

➤ If you really can't muster enough confidence at the moment to say that you are an actor, imagine someone who would find it easy and pretend that you are them: 'My name is Michael Chekhov. I am an actor.' You can choose to be anyone you like!

➤ If this is still too difficult for you, cross the threshold and say whatever you want, but say it with the feeling of something 'well done'.

CONCENTRATION

Concentration means being with something.
(Chekhov 2000: 30)

Exercise 4.4

➤ Notice an object in the room some distance from you – anything will do. Pay attention to its shape and colour. Imagine that there's a current of energy connecting you with the object. Try not to worry about whether or not you're doing it right – however you imagine it is fine. Then imagine that you are standing beside the object and can touch it and lift it, and that your whole body is in contact with it.

➤ Then stop focusing on the object and your connection to it and notice the difference. Repeat the exercise several times until you are clear about the difference between having this imaginary connection and not having it. Be clear about starting and ending the connection.

➤ Try the above exercise with your eyes closed.

➤ Work with a partner and imagine that there's a current of energy connecting you. Explore this connection at different distances as you move around the room. From time to time break the connection and then try to pick it up again.

➤ Listen to the sound of a drum. Notice how it fills the air around you. Pay attention to the way the sound resonates in your body. When the drumming stops, continue listening.

➤ In pairs, get one person to concentrate on an internal melody in silence. The other should try to distract them by singing aloud. There will, of course, be a number of other people singing, so there's quite a few potential sources of distraction. The partner who is silent pays attention to the difference between being concentrated and being distracted. Reverse roles.

SIGNIFICANCE

Chekhov taught that every action could be a 'little piece of art', with a beginning, middle and end. When you finish one action and before you start the next; there is a pause, however slight. In this pause one thing changes into the next, so, although the body may have stopped moving, there is an inner process where one action fades away and the next one begins.

Exercise 4.5

➤ Take off, or put on, a piece of clothing. Begin from a moment of outer stillness. The action emerges from this pause. When you are partway through the action, pause. In the pause you decide whether to continue, stop or return to where you started. End in a pause.

➤ The group forms a semicircle with one person in the centre. The person is asked two questions. In response to the first they say 'yes' or 'no'. In response to the second, they stay or go. Each response comes out of a pause. In the pause you receive the question, make your decision and then respond.

➤ Speak a line to your audience: 'I would my father looked but with my eyes', for example. Begin with a pause, speak the line and then pause to let the audience receive your words. When you feel they have received them, say 'thank you', pause again and, in the pause, make a decision to leave.

THE FOUR BROTHERS

THE FEELING OF EASE

> Heaviness in an artist is an uncreative power.
> (Chekhov 2002: 13)

Exercise 4.6

➤ Remember times in your life when you have felt light, joyful and at ease with the world, and those times when you have felt heavy, miserable and ill at ease. Get a sense of how these different feelings affected your body. Now focus on the sense of ease and lightness. This is Chekhov's starting point for working with the feeling of ease.

➤ Raise your arms into the air, then bring them down, imagining that you are pouring this feeling of lightness and ease into your body. Imagine that your arms begin in the centre of your chest.

➤ Repeat at a quicker tempo.

One thing to notice in this exercise is that we make a conscious choice to focus on the sense of lightness and ease. In order to train ourselves, we need to have the desire and will to learn – this isn't just true in a general sense, but for each specific skill we are trying to develop.

Exercise 4.7

➤ Go down on one knee and then get up with a feeling of ease.

➤ As you go down, raise your arms and, as you come back up, lower them. Repeat more quickly. Increase the speed until you are going as quickly as you can, but still keep the feeling of ease.

➤ Go down to the floor, lie back so that the back of your head touches the floor, then return to standing (repeat several times). Imagine you are as light as a feather.

➤ Begin to walk with this feeling of ease, and with a sense that the legs begin in the chest centre. Gradually increase speed until you are running. Go as quickly as you can, but don't lose the feeling of ease.

➤ Come to a standstill but continue the feeling of ease without moving.

➤ Find a partner. Keeping a sense of ease, begin to fight with each other. Do this without physical contact. Wrestle, or box, keeping as light as you can. If you notice your body becoming stiff, gently bring your focus back to the feeling of ease. Remember to breathe!

The faster we move with our bodies, the more stiff our psychology has a tendency to become, and this, in turn, can lead to a freezing of the body. So, we have to keep the desire to maintain this feeling of lightness and ease. All exercises should be done with the feeling of ease. During any exercise or in performance try to notice when your body stiffens and focus on the feeling of ease for a moment or two.

THE FEELING OF FORM

Again, we need to find the desire to experience form and, as we begin to explore form, we need to remember the feeling of ease. Chekhov suggests that we can access the feeling of form by acting as if we are creating something and engaging ourselves fully in it. Working with the feeling of form also includes paying attention to the beginning and end of our actions. For Chekhov, this means knowing what we are going to do before we do it; something which helps us develop a clear sense of objective. At all times keep a sense of ease and lightness in your work.

Exercise 4.8

➤ Standing still, become aware of your body as a form. Sense it from the outside first, getting a feeling for its outline in space. Then sense it from the inside as a full form. Accept whatever you find without judgement.

➤ Become aware of the different parts of the body as form: the roundness of the head, the shape of the arms and hands, the torso, the legs and the feet. Imagine everything is connected to the centre in the chest.

➤ Pay attention to the fact that, as a human being, you stand on two legs, whereas most other animals spend nearly all of their time on four. Get down on all fours and distribute your weight equally. Notice how this restricts your movement possibilities.

➤ Put your attention in your hands and imagine bringing them together. Try to get as clear a sense as you can of the shape of this action – its beginning, middle and end. When you feel that you're ready, go ahead and move your hands into the position. Try to pay as much attention as you can to the process of moving them.

➤ Visualise separating your hands again and putting them by your side. Do it. Try to get a sense of the shape made by your position being left in the air after you've moved, as if you'd made the gesture in soft clay.

➤ Repeat at least ten times, trying to get a clearer sense of your hands as movable forms and, in the process, keep a sense of the whole body and its form. The major focus is on the hands, but you continue to keep a sense of the form of the whole body and the hands in relation to it.

➤ Explore moving the whole body in and out of a position and getting a sense of the shape that it leaves in the air. Remember to visualise the form clearly before you move.

➤ Once you have explored these exercises, begin to explore travelling, crawling, walking and running, each time seeing the beginning and end of the action in your imagination before you move. As you travel through space, try to get a sense of the shape your body is leaving in the air.

➤ Move into pairs. One partner should take up a position and hold it, while the other adopts a position in harmony with it. When both are in position, each of you should have a sense of the whole composition. Remember the sense of contact – of being connected with your partner – this time, through the form you've created together. When you step out of the sculpture, try to get a sense of the form of the composition left in the air.

➤ Try this exercise in fours, then sixes, then eights. Then try with as many people as there are in the group. You can use as much space as you need, but remember to keep the sense of contact.

➤ Speak the following line twenty times: 'The strangeness of your story put heaviness in me.' Pay attention to the way your mouth forms the words.

➤ Explore saying the same thing with just your hands. You're not trying to mime but to find a way of carving the form of the sentence in the air. Then try it with your whole body. Once you've got a feeling for this, add the words so that speech and movement end at the same time.

➤ Select a chorus from an ancient Greek tragedy or comedy. Each person should take a line and explore it, as above. Then each person can move and speak their line in sequence, imagining their words travelling through the space and making contact with the speaker of the next line.

THE FEELING OF BEAUTY

Exercise 4.9

➤ Begin to move freely, keeping a sense of ease. Move slowly and simply at first and try to sense the pleasure in movement that comes from your body. It might be a quite subtle feeling, but, however subtle it is, welcome it. Notice how it radiates from you, but don't force it – allow it to grow of its own accord and in its own time. This feeling is related to the sense of joy that comes with ease and lightness.

➤ Move more quickly and explore more complex movements, trying to stay in touch with the feeling of beauty. Chekhov gives the example of someone, profoundly engaged in a physical task, flowing effortlessly.

➤ Do any of the previous exercises in which you explored the feelings of ease or form and pay attention to the feeling of beauty.

➤ Wherever you are, inside or outside of the studio, see where you can discover this feeling of beauty. It may come in response to an art work, or a thought, or the shape of a building, or a patch of rust on an old car. It doesn't matter. We're not trying to find 'conventionally' beautiful objects, but the sense of beauty that can arise when we stop criticising and ignoring the world around us. As Chekhov put it:

> One of the characteristics of the creative soul consists of its ability to see and extract beauty from something which a non-creative soul overlooks altogether.

(Chekhov 1983)

Once we have got in touch with the feeling of beauty, we can begin to ask why particular things evoke this feeling in us – this will enable us to bring together our thoughts and our feelings.

THE FEELING OF THE WHOLE/ENTIRETY

Exercise 4.10

➤ Take a few moments to go over your day prior to arriving in the studio. See if you can split it into sections that appear complete in themselves, like little scenes from a play or a movie. Go over these scenes again and again until you get a clear sense of the beginning and end of each scene and how it connects to the one before and after it. Next, try to get a sense of your day so far as a complex whole with a number of distinct and interrelated parts.

➤ Once you have done this, try imagining the rest of your day in the same way. This time you are working, not with what has happened, but imagining the future. Try to imagine the future in as much detail as you have just recalled the past. Link the two, past and future, together to get a sense of the day as a complex whole.

➤ Try the exercise again, this time with your whole life up to this point and then on into the future as far as you can imagine. The sections will inevitably cover larger blocks of time than in the previous exercise, but try to get a sense of their beginnings and ends and how each scene relates to the one before and after it. Try to get a sense of your life's objective – what you're aiming for.

➤ Tell your story to a partner as if it belonged to someone else. Have your partner tell your story back to you as if it were their own. Notice the differences in the way your partner tells your story. Reverse roles.

➤ Break up the road you travel daily into sections and imagine a story in connection with each section. You don't have to be a character in this story, but try to get a clear sense of the characters who are in it. Connect all of the sections up into a single plot.

➤ Read a folk tale or a short story and recreate it in your imagination, being clear about the beginning and end of each segment of the story. Notice how you break the story into different scenes. Do you make a change when a new character enters? When the location changes? When there is a shift in time? When the atmosphere changes? When a significant action is completed? A combination of these? There's no right or wrong way, just try to become aware of what it is that you do. Once you are familiar with what you do, you can explore different ways of approaching the task.

➤ If you are working on a playtext, do the same as you've done with the folk tale. Don't worry about whether your sections correspond to the playwright's.

➤ Separate three people from the group as performers. The rest should form a semicircle as an audience. The three performers are going to cross an imaginary threshold and 'appear' before the audience. They should walk forward four paces, pause, say 'we are here' and then begin to walk back until they cross the threshold and 'disappear'. This is related to the exercise of making and breaking connection, but, although this is an aspect of this exercise, the image of appearing and disappearing is important. Each performer finds their own way of imagining this. You might, for example, imagine moving from darkness into light and back again, or from air into earth; it doesn't matter – the task is to explore this sense of appearing and disappearing without curtains, flats or lights to mark the threshold.

➤ Perform the previous exercise, but as you walk forward raise your hand. There is no particular gesture you have to make, but it is at its fullest extent when you finish the line 'we are here' and begins to disappear as you walk backwards.

➤ Look for the moments of transformation. The energy builds after crossing the threshold until the line is completed. Then there is a pause. In the pause is a moment of transformation. Try to sense the moment to start the process of disappearing, to move backwards. Remember to keep contact with your fellow performers and with the audience and a feeling of the whole.

ATMOSPHERE

Atmosphere, for Chekhov, unites the performers and the audience. Chekhov was concerned that, because actors are often afraid of the audience, the atmosphere is kept behind the 'fourth wall'. If this happens, the performance is dead as far as Chekhov was concerned. When you are creating atmospheres, be generous with them and include the audience!

Exercise 4.11

➤ Pay attention to atmospheres around you in daily life. Notice the different atmospheres of place, of time of day, of weather and of events. Observe groups of people, large and small, and try to get a sense of the atmosphere that surrounds them. Notice your reactions to these atmospheres: how your voice and gesture adjusts, or how you might feel like changing the atmosphere.

➤ When reading plays, novels or short stories, watching live or recorded performance, listening to music or looking at paintings, pay attention to their atmospheres. Notice how the atmospheres are constructed through language, image, colour, rhythm, etc. Observe your reactions to these different atmospheres.

➤ Imagine a scene from a play or a film with a completely different atmosphere. See it in some detail in your imagination.

➤ Find pieces of different coloured lighting gel and look through them. Allow the colour to affect your behaviour and your mood. Notice the different effects that different colours have. If you're feeling creative, you can make spectacles out of wire and masking tape with different coloured lenses.

➤ Stand still and listen to a sound outside the studio. Notice the atmosphere in the workspace.

➤ Imagine the space filled with a chosen atmosphere. Breathe it in. It is all around you. What images come to mind with his atmosphere? Notice them. When the atmosphere has been established, begin to notice your atmosphere. Be patient, allow the reaction to develop in response to the atmosphere. If nothing comes, don't try to force it.

➤ Once the atmosphere is established, begin to speak in harmony with the atmosphere. Allow your voice to change to match the atmosphere. Don't force it. Imagine that the atmosphere supports you. Hold a conversation with a partner. For the moment, don't worry about character or motivation – just focus on keeping voice and actions in harmony with the atmosphere.

➤ Standing at the threshold, the group should divide into two halves (A and B). Group A should cross the threshold into an atmosphere of moonlight, moving to the far end of the space. They should imagine that the air is filled with the atmosphere and that they are breathing it in and back out again. When Group B feel that the atmosphere has been established, they should enter it. Without planning, Group B can then allow the atmosphere to give them a gift. They should take the gift and give it to someone in Group A. It's important not to plan what the gift will be or who it will be given to before entering the atmosphere. Once the gift has been passed on, sense when the task has been completed by the whole group and leave the space. Perform in silence.

➤ Do exercises from other sections, paying attention to atmosphere.

ACTIONS AND QUALITIES

Exercise 4.12

➤ Walk with your hands clenched at your side then walk with your hands very loose and your arms swinging. Switch from one to the other. Pay attention to the difference in feeling between the two.

STACCATO AND LEGATO

Any action can be performed in a staccato or legato manner. In *staccato*, movements are precise and sharp and the body comes to an abrupt stop. In *legato*, movements are fluid and continuous and the body gradually comes to a stop. Once again, remember the four brothers, and especially to keep a feeling of ease when moving in staccato.

Exercise 4.13

➤ Freely explore staccato and legato movements. Make the smallest and the largest movements that you can in each. Notice how it feels to move in these different ways.

➤ Put on and take off a piece of clothing. Do it first in staccato, then legato. Once you have explored it thoroughly, do the action in a combination of staccato and legato. Pay attention also to the moments of transformation and any changes in your feelings.

➤ Take a nursery rhyme and explore speaking it in staccato and legato. Add movements to accompany the voice. Then move in the opposite manner to the voice: if you're speaking the nursery rhyme in staccato, move in legato, and vice versa.

➤ In pairs, one person should speak the nursery rhyme in staccato or legato, while the other moves in response. Then explore moving in opposition, but beginning and ending at the same time.

➤ Each person in the group should be given a word or a short phrase from the nursery rhyme. The group can then speak the rhyme in sequence, either in staccato or legato. Remember the importance of contact.

➤ Return to the chorus exercise and explore in staccato and legato.

MOULDING

Exercise 4.14

➤ Beginning with your hands and gradually including the whole body, mould the air around you as if it were like clay. Make your movements expansive and bold. Imagine each movement leaving a mark in the air. Vary the speed and intensity of your movements, but keep a sense of ease and lightness. When you come to a stop, pay attention to your inner sense of the quality. How does your body feel after moving with a quality of moulding?

➤ Find a partner. Mould the space around each other. Use your whole body. Vary the speed and explore using staccato and legato.

➤ Find a partner some distance from you in space. Mould your way towards each other and then the space around each other in either staccato, or legato. When one is in staccato the other is in legato. Through the contact between you find the moments to swap.

FLOWING

Exercise 4.15

➤ Each movement, while still being clearly shaped, flows like water into the next one. There is a sense of the rhythm of waves swelling, breaking and subsiding. When you come to a stop, pay attention to your inner sense of the quality. How does your body feel after moving with a quality of flowing?

FLYING

Exercise 4.16

➤ Imagine that your whole body is light – that it would only need a gust of wind to lift you off your feet. Each movement you make continues in space, flying away from you. Link your movements together. When you come to a stop, pay attention to your inner sense of the quality. How does your body feel after moving with a quality of flying?

RADIATING

Exercise 4.17

➤ Each movement is done with a sense of intense energy radiating out from the whole body into the space in the direction of the movement. When you come to a stop, pay attention to your inner sense of the quality. How does your body feel after moving with a quality of radiating?

THE THREE SENSATIONS (THE THREE SISTERS)

These three exercises were taught as a group by Chekhov to Jack Colvin in Hollywood.

Exercise 4.18

➤ Explore *balance* through movement: find different points of balance and explore the moments when you lose your balance. Explore the psychological associations of balance and allow them to influence your movement. We might think, for example, of an 'unbalanced personality'. What kind of movement comes up in us in response to that idea? How might a psychologically unbalanced person move? Perhaps their movement is unusually precise. Allow your imagination to come up with different ideas and explore any other associations that the word 'balance' has for you. Explore large and bold balances and extremely subtle ones. Explore balance in different parts of the body.

➤ Explore *floating* movements, like ashes floating upwards or leaves floating to the ground. Explore the psychological associations of floating and allow them to influence your movement. Allow yourself to explore large movements and very subtle ones. Explore floating with different parts of the body.

➤ Explore *falling* in the same manner as balancing and floating. Examine such associations as 'falling asleep' or 'falling in love'. What kind of falling comes to your imagination when you imagine 'falling in love'?

➤ Explore different characters which emerge from balancing, floating and falling.

QUALITIES AND OBJECTS

Exercise 4.19

➤ Take a ball, a stick or a scarf and explore its qualities. Is it heavy or light? Stiff or flexible? How does it move in space? How does it react to being dropped? Spend time finding out as much about the qualities of your object as you can. Explore how you can move with the qualities of your object. How do these qualities affect your feelings? How can you bring these qualities into your voice? Into the way you shape and move your mouth? What kind of character would move and speak like this? Find out as much as you can about the character.

➤ Repeat the exercise with the other objects.

➤ Find different objects and explore their qualities in the same way. This can be done with anything: sources of litter, such as a crisp packet, a plastic bottle or a drinks can; or a stone, a piece of wood or a flower.

➤ Explore different environments and try to discover their qualities. Find out as much as you can and then try to move, make sounds, and speak with these qualities. What kind of character is produced by these environmental qualities? (Note: you will need to be in the specific environment to do this exploration. You can, however, bring what you learn into the studio.)

➤ Imagine lifting an arm. Notice the detail of the movement, such as the height or the position of your elbow, wrist and fingers. Trying not to impose anything, notice any sensation or quality that comes with your imaginary movement. When you have the action clear in as much detail as possible, carry it out. When you have done it, check what you've done against your image. Did you achieve what you set out to achieve?

➤ Repeat the above exercise, but this time add a specific quality. At first, try raising your arm with a quality of caution. Notice any changes that happen in you as a result. Repeat with the qualities of joy, anger, suspicion, fear, sadness, confidence, love, jealousy, tenderness and smoothness.

➤ Move freely, exploring different qualities. Try to get your whole body moving with the specific quality and then, once it's established, change to another one. See how quickly you can move from one quality to the next.

- ➤ Explore moving with the different qualities in staccato and legato.
- ➤ The group should spread out in the space. One person should throw a ball to another with a specific quality, the catcher receiving it with the same quality. Each action is prepared – it has a clear beginning and ending. Keep a sense of contact with the whole group. Everyone needs to be engaged, whether or not they are the thrower or catcher at that particular moment.
- ➤ Speak a word or a sentence when throwing or receiving.

ARCHETYPAL GESTURES

Exercise 4.20

- ➤ Expand into a star shape, saying to yourself 'I am going to awaken the sleeping muscles of my body.' When you reach the physical limit of your expansion, imagine that the movement is continuing. When you reach the limit of your imagination, return to your starting position and repeat.
- ➤ Contract inwards and downwards, crossing your arms across your chest, bowing your head and going down on to your knees. Imagine that the space around you is contracting also. When you have reached your physical limit, imagine that you are continuing to contract. When you have reached the limit of your imagination, return to your starting position and repeat.
- ➤ Explore the actions of expanding and contracting while speaking the line 'I want to be left alone!' Try to speak in harmony with the gesture and notice the effects the different gestures have on your speech.
- ➤ Repeat the actions of expanding and contracting. When you return to your starting point after each movement, pause and feel the sensation of the action reverberating inside you. In the pause, allow this echo to fade and transform into the impulse for the next movement.
- ➤ In the pause, with your attention still on the reverberation of the action inside, speak your line. There is no outer action. Notice the difference between speaking from the sensation of expansion and from the sensation of contraction.
- ➤ This time do the action fully in your imagination only, and then speak the line.

➤ This is the basic idea of the psychological gesture. Two 'characters' have the same lines, but the inner gesture for each is different. One is expanding and the other is contracting. One is increasing in size, taking space away from others, the other is reducing in size and hiding from others. Although both have the same objective, to be left alone, they express it differently. This time do the action entirely in your imagination as you speak the line.

➤ Explore as many different ways of contracting and expanding your whole body as you can, remembering to continue the action in your imagination once your physical limit is reached. Each time sense the results of the action reverberating in your body once you return to the starting position.

➤ Explore expanding and contracting with different parts of the body.

➤ Explore gestures of pulling, pushing, lifting, throwing, tearing, embracing, closing, penetrating, slashing, smashing, opening and wringing. Make each gesture as full and as clear as possible, involving your whole body in the space. (Notice how, in order to do a number of these actions, you have to start by moving in the opposite direction.) When you reach the physical limit of any action, imagine your gesture continuing beyond your body. Pause after each movement. Explore one way of doing a gesture in some detail and then explore other ways. See how many different kinds of pushes, for example, you can you come up with, but remember to make each full and clear.

➤ Explore each gesture in terms of its psychological associations, as you did for balance, floating and falling.

➤ Explore each gesture in staccato and legato.

➤ Repeat each gesture, beginning slowly and accelerating towards the end, continuing the acceleration in your imagination once the movement has reached its limit.

➤ Repeat each gesture, starting quickly and slowing down towards the end.

➤ Repeat each gesture, allowing a sound to emerge as an accompaniment. Experiment with different durations. When the movement has reached its physical limit, take the sound inwards as well; or the opposite: when the movement reaches its limit continue to make the sound aloud to accompany the movement in your imagination.

➤ Repeat each gesture, allowing a phrase to emerge. Notice how different gestures bring different kinds of verbal responses from you.

➤ Speak the same piece of text to accompany each gesture. Notice how the different gestures alter your experience of the text. Next, do the gesture purely internally while speaking the text. You can do this with a nursery rhyme or with the words of a song, if you don't have a speech to hand. Try to keep the same amount of energy in your internal gesture as there was in your full-bodied external one.

➤ Repeat the gestures while adding different qualities. Choose three or four different qualities to begin with and spend some time exploring each one thoroughly, noticing your feelings. Then explore moving from one quality to another, making the changes as clearly and as quickly as possible.

➤ In pairs, explore a short piece of dialogue using contrasting gestures: for example, push/pull, open/close, penetrate/embrace. At first, explore using the whole body gesture and gradually decrease the size of the external gesture until it becomes purely internal. Try to do this without any loss of energy or power. Take time to receive the impulse from your partner, taking in their action on you before you initiate your contrasting movement. Once you've explored this thoroughly, switch roles. Then explore different gestures with your text. Don't forget the work you've done on contact.

Example:

A pushes: 'I didn't expect to see you here.'
B pulls: 'I didn't expect to see you here either.'

A embraces : 'How are you?'
B penetrates: 'Very well, how are you?'

➤ Throughout all of these exercises on archetypal gestures, notice the characters that will begin to emerge in your imagination and record them in words and images, so that you can work with them some more in the future.

IMAGINATION

Exercise 4.21

➤ Imagine a flower in as much detail as you can. Do different activities, keeping this image of a flower, and notice how it affects your movement and your voice. Repeat, using different images: a snake, a knife, a warm bed or an angry wasp, for example. Anything you can come up with is fine, as long as you imagine it in as much detail as you can.

➤ Imagine a frog turning into a prince, a seed growing into a tree, a bird changing into an elephant, a table turning into a bear, or a tower metamorphosing into a carnation. Try these and add any others that you can think of. Imagine the changes in as much detail as you can – try not to jump over the difficult bits, but wait attentively for your imagination to solve the problem.

➤ Imagine yourself transforming into something else. See your body as clearly as you can and imagine each stage of the change. Don't forget to imagine the change in your psychology. Then try to physicalise what you've imagined. When you are ready, imagine yourself changing back again.

➤ Imagine someone who is very different from you – someone who is able to do things that you can't. Imagine yourself being transformed into that person and explore what it's like to be them from this perspective. When you're ready, imagine yourself changing back again.

➤ Look for resemblances between objects and people. If this object were a person, what kind of character would they be? And the reverse: if this person were an object, what kind of object would they be? Explore this in your imagination and then in movement and sound.

➤ Look for resemblances between animals and people. If this animal were a person, what kind of character would they be? If this person were an animal, what kind of animal would they be? Explore this in your imagination and then in movement and sound.

➤ Take any everyday action and repeat it at least twenty times, but make it different each time. Any action will do, sitting down, taking off or putting on a piece of clothing, opening a door, picking up a pen. Try to avoid any repetition.

CENTRES

Exercise 4.22

➤ 'Imagine a Center in your chest from which living impulses are sent out into your arms, hands, legs and feet. Start to move, imagining that the impulse to form the movement comes from this Center' (Chekhov 1991: 44). Explore moving around the room, imagining that the energy that flows from this centre releases any blocks that you may have in your hips, knees, ankles, elbows and wrists. Try it with large gestures and very small ones, keeping a sense of the impulse coming from the chest centre.

➤ Place an imaginary centre anywhere in your body. It can be in your big toe or the base of your spine, between the eyes or the inside of your elbow. It can even be outside of your body, above your head, in front of your eyes and always slightly out of reach. There are no limits to where you can imagine the centre. Once you have got a clear sense of where it is, imagine that all of your movements and actions begin with an impulse from this centre. What kind of character emerges when you work from this centre? Explore four or five different centres to begin with, returning to the chest centre after each one.

➤ In the previous exercise you were only asked to place the centre and imagine that impulses came from it. This time apply your imagination to the qualities of the centre itself. Is it mobile or static? Fast or slow? Bright or dull? Soft or hard? Expanding or contracting? Does it have a colour? A texture? There are no limits to how you can imagine the centre. Once you begin to move, notice how the qualities of the centre affect your movement and your psychology. What kind of character are you embodying? Try to find a voice for your character. Remember to return your focus to the chest centre at the end of the exercise.

➤ If you place the centre in the same place, but change its qualities, how does this affect the kind of character that emerges? How does it affect your movement and voice?

➤ Explore interacting with other people from your imaginary centre and notice what happens. As your character begins to emerge, try to notice what it wants from other people. What is its objective?

➤ Describe your imaginary centre to a partner. If you explore working from each other's imaginary centres, do the same characters emerge?

➤ In approaching the centre from this direction we've allowed a character to emerge from the centre. We can also go the other way round and start with a character and try to find the centre that belongs to it. Take any play or story that you know well and imagine a scene from it in as much detail as you can. Try to find out where each character's centre is and get a sense of its qualities. One way of doing this is to enter into an imaginary dialogue with the character and ask: 'Please show me where your centre is. ... What qualities does it have?'

➤ Observe people in public places and try to guess placement and qualities of their centres. Make a note of what you guess and explore working from this material in the studio.

ARCHETYPES

In several exercises I've suggested that you notice the 'kind' of character that's emerging. I could have said 'type' instead. Thinking in 'kinds' or 'types' is a way of organising our experience, of putting things that have similar qualities together. You might answer the question, 'What kind of character?', with 'A kind of (or a type of) Warrior'. The next question would be 'What kind of Warrior?' and you might answer 'A kind of woman warrior'. You can imagine the questioning continuing ('What kind of woman warrior', etc.) and more information being revealed. We have a large type, Warrior, and then a subtype, 'woman warrior', which itself can be broken down into smaller units. One way of thinking is to call the larger type an 'archetype'. The archetype includes all of the possibilities that could make up a character of that type. The archetype itself can't easily be imagined, because any specific image necessarily excludes something. In this instance, if the character is a 'woman warrior', she can't be a 'man warrior'. If the term 'man warrior' sounds odd, it's because we generally think of warriors being men rather than women.

Earlier we explored archetypal gestures (push, pull, etc.). We didn't try to identify a push, for example, that was an archetype. We started from one particular example of pushing and the freely explored different kinds of pushing. We approach an understanding of the archetype through a sense of what links these various actions together. It is helpful to think of archetypal characters in this way too.

Here are some figures which have been referred to as archetypes: the Child, the Stepmother, the Stepfather, the Warrior, the Saint, the Critic, the Devil, the Monster, the Killer, the King, the Queen, the Fool, the Adolescent, the Magician, the Hero/Heroine, the Innocent, the Prostitute, the Lover, the Mother, the Father, the Cook, the Dragon, the Giant, the Witch and the Addict.

If we were to say that there was only one way of representing a Fool, and that it must always be done in this way, whatever the play and whatever the circumstances, we would be moving towards a stereotype. Stereotypes are a way of ignoring difference and limiting expression. The aim in Chekhov's work is to identify the archetype as a way of getting different information about the character and as a way of expanding our conception. If we say 'All fathers are the same . . .', we're probably stereotyping.

We can start by identifying the archetype and then making our character more and more individual, according to what's necessary for the style of the play. An individual character might be a mixture of different archetypal characters (Queen and Heroine and Lover, for example), although one may be dominant.

When we are exploring archetypes we are always looking for something that is larger than what we see in everyday life.

Exercise 4.23

➤ Choose an archetypal figure from the list above. See this figure in your imagination in as much detail as possible. Once you can see the figure quite clearly, stop. Start again, choosing the same archetype, but imagining it as differently as you can from your first attempt. Repeat this several times until you begin to get a sense of the difference between the archetype itself and each related individual.

IMAGINARY BODIES

We've already been working with imaginary bodies in some of the earlier exercises. Chekhov was always interested in the difference between the actor and the character and working with imaginary bodies is a way of engaging with that difference. By taking on different characteristics, a skilled actor can seem taller, narrower, shorter or broader than they actually are.

Exercise 4.24

➤ Think of any imaginary body. You can choose from the list of archetypes if you like, or it could be a character from a play, film, novel or folk tale, or something purely from your imagination. You can also use figures and shapes from paintings.

➤ Visualise the body as clearly as you can in your imagination. Ask the figure 'leading questions' to get more details (e.g. 'Let me see your hands', 'Show me how you run to meet a loved one'). Get a sense of the whereabouts and quality of the figure's centre. If getting a sense of the centre is difficult, choose one at random and attribute any qualities to it – you can always change later if you feel the character wants something else.

➤ Visualise the imaginary body standing beside you, and notice the difference between it and yourself. Step inside the imaginary body, allowing your self-image to shift so that it is as close as you can get to the figure's. You can start by taking on a part of the body first, rather than trying to take it on all at once. Explore to find out which way works best for you.

➤ Now get a sense of the kind of character you've created. Begin to move as the character, find appropriate sounds and, when you're ready, begin to speak. Explore different activities as the character until you can move and speak quite easily. It's not unusual to be quite stiff at first as you learn to move in the new body. Try to remember the feeling of ease.

➤ In the next thirty minutes, create five distinct characters.

OBJECTIVES AND THE PSYCHOLOGICAL GESTURE

Exercise 4.25

➤ Your objective is simple. You want to get to the nearest wall. Unfortunately you can't move. Explore!

➤ Select some simple objectives: 'I want to get out', 'I want to hear every little thing', 'I want to solve the problem', 'I want to be left alone' or 'I want someone to help me'. Choose one at a time and find a full-body gesture that expresses this objective for you. If it helps, you can start with your hands first, but try to feel your way into the gesture, rather than building it up by analysing the objective. Speak the words that accompany the gesture.

➤ Once you've found your gesture, you can explore it in the various ways in which you examined your archetypal gestures earlier. Notice how the various changes affect your feelings and the way you speak your objective. Certain variations might change the objective. Put those aside – they're no use to you.

➤ Practise doing your gesture internally, trying to keep the same qualities and energy as when you did it outwardly.

➤ Improvise a scene with a partner. You are in a situation in which neither of you can leave. Keep your objective throughout the improvisation, but don't speak it unless it really seems the most appropriate thing to do at that moment. Staying connected with your inner gesture, see if you can make your outer behaviour contrast with it.

➤ Working with a character from a story or a play, go through the events of the whole piece in your imagination, seeing your character among the others and in the various environments. Try to get a sense of what the character's main desire is. What is it that this character wants? When you get a sense of this, even if it's just a faint hint and something you're not sure that you can put into words, begin to make a gesture with just your hand and arm. Allow it to develop, staying in touch with your sense of the character, and gradually allow the gesture to spread to the whole body. As the gesture develops and spreads, you may want to make changes as the character's desire becomes more clear to you. This is the 'psychological gesture' (PG).

➤ Although you've found the dominant desire of your character and have turned it into a PG, the character will also have other desires and objectives in the course of the play, or even in the course of a single speech. You can explore your character's wants at different moments and turn them into PG. The PG for the entire character will influence how you do these minor PGs.

ENSEMBLE AND GROUP SCULPTURES

We've already explored a number of group exercises. Here are some additional ones. Don't forget the sense of ease, form, beauty and entirety, or the sense of contact. Remember to use atmosphere in your group sculptures and to radiate it out to the audience.

Exercise 4.26

➤ One person takes up a position in response to a given theme (e.g. grief, liberty, bondage) and a second person takes up a position in relation to it, enhancing the theme.

➤ Repeat the exercise above, but with four people. Remember to keep a sense of contact and of the whole.

➤ Repeat with the whole group.

➤ Construct a group sculpture around a chosen theme (e.g. victory, peace, war, revenge) and style (comedy, tragedy, melodrama, clown). From the edges of the space each actor moves towards the place where the sculpture is to be made. As the group begins to come together the members adjust to each other to construct the sculpture. Each person tries to have a sense of the whole sculpture and their place within it. When the sculpture is complete, hold it for a few slow breaths and then let it go as a group. Sense the moment. In the previous sculpting exercise people joined one at a time; in this one the sculpture takes shape from the group as a whole.

➤ Explore the minimum amount of alteration to shift the sculpture from one style to another (e.g. from comedy to tragedy).

➤ Listen to a piece of music and let the sculpture emerge in response to it.

➤ Get the group to stand in a circle and make contact, everyone letting out a sustained 'ahh' sound. Try to start and end at the same moment. Repeat, but this time move away from the circle on the sound and stop moving when the sound stops. Keep a sense of the whole group throughout this. From the pause, find the moment to move back to the circle together as a group. The return happens in silence.

➤ Find your own space and lie on the floor. Synchronise your breathing with the rest of the group. Send your breath to the member of the group who is furthest from you and listen to their breath.

REHEARSAL

Any of the above exercises can, of course, be used as part of the rehearsal or devising process. Chekhov had his students devising work on the basis of folk tales, and we have seen that *The Possessed* was to some extent a devised piece. When Chekhov writes about the process of putting on a performance, however, he generally writes about working on a traditional playtext. Most of the exercises that follow assume that you are staging a pre-scripted play, are devising on the basis of a pre-existent story, or that the shape of your devised performance is already reasonably clear.

In the rehearsal process Chekhov advised against working on the piece in a systematic linear fashion, but recommended a detailed work on key moments that function as 'attractors' for the rest of the action. An awareness of the place of these moments within the whole needs to be kept in mind.

Exercise 4.27

➤ Read the text two or three times and get a sense of the general atmosphere and the different atmospheres that are framed by it (a comedy has a different general atmosphere from a tragedy). Atmospheres provide the 'soul' of the performance, so it is important to get into the feeling world of the story. What images come to mind? What sounds? Smells? Tastes? Feelings? Get a sense of the storyline, the characters and the social significance of the piece. Don't try to answer the questions through a logical approach – allow your imagination time to work. Begin a notebook for your impressions.

➤ Make a score of the atmospheres for your piece. Pay attention to the moments of transformation.

➤ Consider your piece, paying attention to its form. What are the three major sections of the performance and their moments of greatest tension? What are the opposing forces in the conflict? What are the key changes that take place? Note down what you discover.

➤ Pay attention to the rhythmic ebb and flow of energy in your performance.

➤ Notice those elements of the performance that repeat. What is the aim of the repetition? Is what's repeated always the same, or does it reappear in modified form? What effect will the repetition have on the audience?

➤ Explore sequences from your performance in different styles. If it's a tragedy, play the scenes with the most suffering as comedy or farce. Whatever style you've been working in, look for the opposite.

➤ Explore scenes in the style of a TV soap, a horror movie, naturalism, expressionism, dada, physical theatre or melodrama.

➤ What is the audience going to get from this piece? Why do it? What is its relevance to what's happening in the world?

BIBLIOGRAPHY

BOOKS AND JOURNALS

Barba, Eugenio (1995) *The Paper Canoe*, London and New York: Routledge.

Benedetti, Jean (1990) *Stanislavski: A Biography*, London: Methuen.

Black, Lendley (1987) *Mikhail Chekhov as Actor, Director, and Teacher*, Ann Arbor, MI: UMI Research Press.

Braun, Edward (ed.) (1978) *Meyerhold on Theatre*, London: Eyre Methuen.

Bridgmont, Peter (1992) *Liberation of the Actor*, London: Temple Lodge.

Byckling, Liisa (1995) 'Pages from the Past: *The Possessed* Produced by Michael Chekhov on Broadway in 1939', *Slavic and East European Performance* 15(2): 32–45.

Chamberlain, Franc (2000) 'Michael Chekhov on the Technique of Acting', in Alison Hodge (ed.) *Twentieth-Century Actor Training*, London: Routledge, pp. 79–97.

Chekhov, Michael (1928) *Put'aktera* [The Path of the Actor], Leningrad: Asadiea. (Unpublished trans. Blaxland-Delange, Simon (2000).)

Chekhov, Michael (1939) 'Pickwick' (unpublished ms.), Dartington Hall Trust Archive, Dartington, UK.

Chekhov, Michael (1942) 'To the Actor' (unpublished version), Dartington Hall Trust Archive, Dartington, UK.

Chekhov, Michael (1983) 'Chekhov on Acting: A Collection of Unpublished Materials', *The Drama Review* 27(3): 46–83.

Chekhov, Michael (1985) *Lessons for the Professional Actor*, New York: PAJ Books.

Chekhov, Michael (1988) 'The Golden Age of the Russian Theatre', *Alarums and Excursions* 2, Los Angeles.

Chekhov, Michael (1991) *On the Technique of Acting*, New York: Harper Perennial.

Chekhov, Michael (2000) *Lessons for Teachers of his Acting Technique*, Ottawa: Dovehouse Editions.

Chekhov, Michael (2002) *To the Actor*, London: Routledge.

Cole, Toby and Chinoy, Helen Krich (eds) (1963) *Directors on Directing: A Source Book of the Modern Theatre*, New York: Bobbs-Merrill Company.

Craig, Edward Gordon (1980) *On the Art of the Theatre*, London: Heinemann Educational Books.

The Drama Review (1983) 'Michael Chekhov's Career and Legacy', *The Drama Review* 27(3): whole issue.

du Prey, Deirdre Hurst (1978) *The Training Sessions of Michael Chekhov*, Dartington: Dartington Theatre Papers.

du Prey, Deirdre Hurst (1983) 'Working With Chekhov', *The Drama Review* 27(3): 84–90.

Gielgud, John (1937) 'Review of *An Actor Prepares*', *Theatre Arts Monthly*, January: 31–4.

Gordon, Mel (1987) *The Stanislavsky Technique: Russia. A Workbook for Actors*, New York: Applause Books.

Gordon, Mel (1995) '*The Castle Awakens*: Mikhail Chekhov's 1931 Occult Fantasy', *Performing Arts Journal* 49: 113–20.

Green, Michael (1986) *The Russian Symbolist Theatre: An Anthology of Plays and Critical Texts,* Ann Arbor, MI: Ardis.

Hodge, Alison (ed.) (2000) *Twentieth-Century Actor Training*, London: Routledge.

Hornby, Richard (1992) *The End of Acting: A Radical View*, New York: Applause.

Innes, Christopher (1998) *Edward Gordon Craig: A Vision of the Theatre*, Amsterdam: Harwood Academic Press.

Kirillov, Andrei (1994) 'Michael Chekhov – Problems of Study', *Eye of the World* 1, St Petersburg.

Leach, Robert (1997) 'When He Touches Your Heart . . .: The Revolutionary Theatre of Vsevolod Meyerhold and the Development of Michael Chekhov', *Contemporary Theatre Review* 7(1): 67–83.

Leonard, Charles (1984) *Michael Chekhov's* To the Director and Playwright, New York: Limelight Editions.

Powers, Mala (2002) 'The Past, Present and Future of Michael Chekhov', in Michael Chekhov *To the Actor*, London: Routledge, pp. xxv–xlviii.

Raffe, Marjorie, Harwood, Cecil and Lundgren, Marguerite (1974) *Eurythmy and the Impulse of Dance*, London: Rudolf Steiner Press.

Senelick, Laurence (1981) *Russian Dramatic Theory from Pushkin to the Symbolists*, Austin: University of Texas Press.

Stanislavsky, Constantin (1980) *An Actor Prepares*, London: Eyre Methuen.

Steiner, Rudolf (1960) *Speech and Drama*, London: Rudolf Steiner Press.

Steiner, Rudolf (1964) *Knowledge of the Higher Worlds and its Attainment*, Mokelumne Hill, CA: Health Research.

Vakhtangov, Eugene (1922) 'Fantastic Realism', in Toby Cole and Helen Krich Chinoy (eds) (1963) *Directors on Directing: A Source Book of the Modern Theatre*, New York: Bobbs-Merrill Company, pp. 185–91.

VIDEO

Mason, Felicity (1993) *The Training Sessions of Michael Chekhov*, Exeter: Arts Documentation Unit.

Merlin, Joanna (2000) *Michael Chekhov's Psychological Gesture*, Exeter: Arts Documentation Unit.

Sharp, Martin (2002) *Michael Chekhov: The Dartington Years*, Hove: Palomino Films.

AUDIO TAPES

Grove, Eddy (1992) *The Nature and Significance of Michael Chekhov's Contribution to the Theory and Technique of Acting*, New York: Eddy Grove.

Powers, Mala (1992) *Michael Chekhov: On Theatre and the Art of Acting: A Guide to Discovery with Exercises*, New York: Applause.

USEFUL WEBSITES

www.michaelchekhov.net

www.michaelchekhov.org.uk

INDEX

eBooks

eBooks – at www.eBookstore.tandf.co.uk

A library at your fingertips!

eBooks are electronic versions of printed books. You can store them on your PC/laptop or browse them online.

They have advantages for anyone needing rapid access to a wide variety of published, copyright information.

eBooks can help your research by enabling you to bookmark chapters, annotate text and use instant searches to find specific words or phrases. Several eBook files would fit on even a small laptop or PDA.

NEW: Save money by eSubscribing: cheap, online access to any eBook for as long as you need it.

Annual subscription packages

We now offer special low-cost bulk subscriptions to packages of eBooks in certain subject areas. These are available to libraries or to individuals.

For more information please contact webmaster.ebooks@tandf.co.uk

We're continually developing the eBook concept, so keep up to date by visiting the website.

www.eBookstore.tandf.co.uk

ROUTLEDGE STUDY GUIDES

WORK SMARTER, NOT HARDER

It's a simple fact - everyone needs a bit of help with their stu
Whether you are studying for academic qualifications (from A-leve
doctorates), undertaking a professional development course or
require good, common sense advice on how to write an essay o
together a coherent and effective report or project, Routledge S
Guides can help you realise your full potential.

Our impressive range of titles covers the following areas:

- Speaking
- Science
- Doctorate

- Study Technique
- English
- MBA

- Thinking
- History
- Research

- Writing
- Mathematics

- Politics

**Available at all good bookshops or you can visit
website to browse and buy Routledge Study Gui
online at:**

www.study-guides.cor
www.study-guides.cor
www.study-guides.cor
www.study-guides.cor
www.study-guides.cor

ROUTLEDGE